Export Instability and Compensatory Financing

In a volatile world economy, developing countries are vulnerable to changes in the international trading environment, particularly in the level of commodity prices. Indeed much money has been spent by national and international organizations compensating producers and countries for shortfalls in export earnings as a result of such instability. Much has been written on the adverse effects of export instability on economic growth. Yet there is no comprehensive account of these effects or of the success of the existing compensatory financing facilities in dealing with them.

Export Instability and Compensatory Financing fills this gap. Its timing is appropriate as there have been calls to establish additional compensatory financing schemes. After examining the operations of the International Monetary Fund's compensatory financing facility and the European Community's Stabex scheme, the author concludes that the case for an additional scheme along the lines suggested by UNCTAD is not clear. The problem of export instability should not be seen as an integral part of the general problem of economic underdevelopment and should be dealt with by a broadly based programme concerned with creating greater growth and stability. This implies not the establishment of an additional facility, but rather that the IMF, the World Bank and other international organizations pay adequate attention to the instability issue in their adjustment programmes for developing countries.

David Lim is Dean of the Division of Asian and International Studies at Griffith University, Brisbane, Australia. He has published extensively on many areas of Development Economics, particularly as they relate to his native Malaysia. He has also served as a consultant to many international organizations dealing with economic development.

Export Instability and Compensatory Financing

David Lim

London and New York

First published 1991
by Routledge
11 New Fetter Lane, London EC4P 4EE

Simultaneously published in the USA and Canada
by Routledge
a division of Routledge, Chapman and Hall, Inc.
29 West 35th Street, New York, NY 10001

Printed and bound in Great Britain by
Mackays of Chatham PLC, Chatham, Kent

British Library Cataloguing in Publication Data

Lim, David
Export instability and compensatory financing.
1. Developing countries. Exporting. Foreign assistance
I. Title
382.60951

ISBN 0-415-03645-3

Library of Congress Cataloging in Publication Data
Lim, David.
Export instability and compensatory financing / David Lim.
p. cm.
"November 1989."
Includes bibliographical references and index.
ISBN 0-415-03645-3
1. Exports-Developing countries-Finance. 2. Balance of trade-Developing countries. 3. Compensatory financing-Developing countries. 4. International Monetary Fund. 5. Developing countries-Commercial policy. 6. Economic development. I. Title.
HF1413.L54 1990 90-43183
382'.17'091724-dc20 CIP

To Sue for her unwavering support

Contents

Tables

Figures

Appendices

Preface

This book is the result of many years of interest in the effect of export instability on economic growth. It began in 1966 when, as a graduate student in England, I was asked to write, for an assignment, a review of the newly published book, *Export Instability and Economic Growth*, by Alaisdair MacBean. I was struck then by the spirited and readable way in which the book challenged the conventional wisdom of that time - that export instability was very high in primary-producing developing countries and was very harmful to their economic growth. In the years that followed I was also struck by the determined way in which the conventional wisdom was defended and the sometimes vitriolic way in which MacBean's work was reviewed.

In 1970 I returned to work in a university in Malaysia. In the preparation of lecture-notes on the Malaysian economy, I had to go through the literature on the relationship between export instability and economic growth and assess its relevance for Malaysia. On the surface, the export-oriented Malaysian economy with its heavy reliance on rubber and tin, products known for their unstable prices, would have been very adversely affected by export instability. However, whatever empirical work there was on Malaysia showed otherwise. This was a surprise. Another was that some of the international empirical work left much to be desired. Often the samples of countries used in cross-country analyses were inappropriate and the models used inconsistent with the hypotheses to be tested.

All this led me to carry out my own research on the matter, beginning with Malaysia and later extending to other countries. Possibly because of this work I was invited in 1984 to be a member of an Expert Group on the compensatory financing of shortfalls in export earnings, established by the United Nations Conference on Trade and Development (UNCTAD). This group, which consisted of nineteen members from nineteen countries, met a number of times in 1984 and, with the assistance of the UNCTAD Secretariat, produced its report in early 1985. In the work for the report I learned much about compensatory financing from the other members of the expert group and from those members of the UNCTAD Secretariat concerned with commodity issues.

In 1986 I prepared a report for the Economic and Social Policy Department of the Food and Agriculture Organization on the operation of the International Monetary Fund's compensatory financing facility.

This study put me in touch with the views of an international organization concerned with the effects of price fluctuations on agricultural production, but which has not been, unlike UNCTAD, in the forefront of the debate. It also enabled me to review my thoughts on the effects of export instability on economic growth and to revise my views somewhat on the need for another compensatory financing facility.

As can be seen, I am indebted to many individuals and organizations in the evolution of my thinking on the subject matter of this book. On a more immediate level, I am grateful to Robyn White for the skilful, efficient and cheerful production of the camera-ready copy of the manuscript, Pat Trigger for uncomplaining research assistance and Hilary Martyn for keeping at bay colleagues eating into scarce writing time. I would also like to thank Peter Sowden and Alan Jarvis for encouraging the project through to the publication stage. My wife Sue, was a tower of strength during the writing of this book, which took place under very difficult circumstances. To her I owe the most and to her I dedicate this book.

David Lim
Griffith University
Brisbane
Queensland
AUSTRALIA 4111

Part I
Export Instability and Economic Growth

1
Introduction

In recent years, discussion of the constraints on the economic development of resource-rich developing countries has centred on the problems created by the so-called Dutch Disease, where the existence of a buoyant export sector is seen to be a bane rather than a boon in the long run (Corden, 1984).

There is an older and equally important issue associated with developing countries that are rich in primary resources and that depend heavily on a few primary products for export. This is the issue of the high degree of instability in the export earnings from these primary commodities and the adverse effect that this may have on the growth of the developing countries concerned. This issue goes back to the early part of the 1950s when the Korean War boom produced development effects which seemed to support the worst fears of a number of United Nations studies (1951 and 1952), and prompted a number of academic studies which further testified to the detrimental effects of export instability on economic growth (Myrdal, 1956; Nurkse, 1953).

This study looks at the nature of the relationship between export instability and economic growth and the attempts by the International Monetary Fund Compensatory Financing Facility (IMF-CFF) and the European Community's Stabex to deal with the presumed adverse effects of instability on growth. Chapter 2 examines the degree and the causes of export instability in primary-producing developing countries. Chapter 3 presents the *a priori* arguments that export instability is detrimental to economic growth, and the results of the empirical verification of these arguments.

The purpose of Chapters 2 and 3, which form Part I of the study, is to establish that it is export earnings, rather than prices, that require stabilizing; that instability in export earnings will harm economic growth and that this detrimental effect is felt through a number of quite different channels. There is little point in setting up the IMF-CFF or any other scheme with the specific purpose of mitigating the adverse effects of export instability on economic growth, without a firm idea of the variable to be stabilized and without having established that export instability is indeed detrimental to economic growth. It is also important to identify the different ways that export instability can harm the process of economic growth, so that the adequacy of the existing compensatory financing schemes to deal with the entire range of economic ills emanating from instability can be assessed properly.

Part II of this study deals with the IMF-CFF and Stabex and their ability to reduce the harmful effect of export instability on the development planning process. Chapter 4 describes the IMF-CFF and its operation since its establishment in 1963. Chapter 5 then assesses the impact that the facility has in stabilizing export earnings, in dealing with the causes of instability and in neutralizing the adverse effects of instability on growth. Chapter 6 describes Stabex and its operations since 1975, when it was set up. Chapter 7 examines its record in achieving its stated aim of remedying the harmful effects of instability in export earnings.

Part III examines the case for an additional compensatory financing facility. Chapter 8 describes the additional facility suggested by UNCTAD and Chapter 9 assesses the viability of such a scheme and shows how some of the existing international arrangements can be and have been modified to cope with the purported adverse effects of export instability.

2
Degree and Causes of Export Instability

Degree of Export Instability

The instability of export earnings refers to the short-term variations of the earnings from the trend over a given period. It thus includes the positive and negative deviations of export earnings from the trend, and it is the impact of both types of deviations on economic growth that is being studied. To examine only the effect of shortfalls in primary commodity earnings (i.e. the negative deviations from the trend) on economic growth is to be concerned largely with the impact of a decline in the commodity terms of trade on growth. While the terms of trade issue is important, it must not be confused with the one on export instability. The former is concerned with the impact of adverse movements in the relative price trend on economic growth, the latter with the impact of revenue fluctuations around the trend on economic growth. This study is concerned with the latter, which can exist even if the trend were to be upward.

It is also important to note that stability in export earnings is not the same as stability in prices under all circumstances. Fluctuations in export earnings can be caused by fluctuations in export prices or export quantities or both. If prices are kept completely stable by the operation of, say, an international commodity agreement, unstable export earnings, caused by fluctuations in the quantities exported, will be made more stable, only if supply is price inelastic and the price elasticity of demand is less than half (Kanbur, 1986). However, partial price stabilization will reduce earnings instability if supply is price inelastic and the price elasticity of demand is less than one (Nguyen, 1980). It is also generally agreed that if price fluctuations are brought about entirely by shifts in demand, then price stabilization will stabilize export earnings. For such a demand-shift market, the influence of the size of the price elasticity of demand on the ability of price stabilization to reduce earnings instability will be decreased considerably.

As will become evident later on, the literature on the relationship between export instability and economic growth shows that it is stability in earnings rather than prices that matters in the debate. It is also clear from the general literature on commodity price stabilization (Newbery and Stiglitz, 1981) that, on a micro and macro basis, income instability is of more concern to economic entities than price instability. Moreover, from the point of view of economic welfare, the important variable may be consumption and not income. In this study, export instability refers to instability in export earnings.

There are many different ways of estimating the trend and therefore of measuring instability in export earnings (Stein, 1977; Lawson, 1974; Leith, 1970). However, no matter how instability is measured, it is generally agreed that the export earnings of those developing countries which depend on primary products are rather unstable and certainly more so than the export earnings of countries, whether rich or poor, which depend on manufactured goods. In general, developing countries experience significantly greater fluctuations in export earnings than developed countries, largely because they depend more on the export of primary products.

An early pioneering study of international economic instability, by Coppock (1962), shows that the instability index of the export proceeds of forty-five developing countries (23.1) was greater than that for eighteen developed countries (17.6) for the period 1946-58. Erb and Schiavo-Campo (1969), using the Coppock instability index, found that although the mean index for the export earnings of both groups of countries had fallen over the more recent period, 1954-66, the mean for the developing countries was nearly 100 per cent higher than that for developed countries.

Studies by Massell (1970), Lawson (1974), Naya (1973), Glezakos (1973), and Kenen and Voivodas (1972) confirmed the results of the earlier studies that the export earnings of developing countries fluctuated significantly more than those for developed countries in the 1950s and 1960s. The difference was also observed by Lancieri (1978) and UNCTAD (1985) to have continued into the 1970s and the early part of the 1980s. Perhaps equally important is the finding by the UNCTAD study that the absolute level of export instability for developing countries had increased over the period 1962-81.

Causes of Export Instability

It is generally accepted that if the export commodities concerned have low price elasticities of supply and demand and encounter large and frequent shifts in their supply and demand, then their export earnings will fluctuate significantly. It is also widely accepted that the supply and demand conditions in the primary commodity sector approximate these conditions closely, and that shifts in supply are more important than shifts in demand in destabilizing export earnings at the country level.

Price elasticities
The price elasticities of supply of agricultural products, especially those of perennial crops, and of mineral products are considerably less than one (Behrman, 1968). The values obtained for the rubber and tin producers of Malaysia for the 1960s (0.12 and 0.20, respectively) are typical, and reflect the inherent lags in supply responses found in the production of most primary commodities (Lim, 1975). At the same time, the price elasticities of demand for primary commodities are also low as the demand is a derived one in which the cost of the primary commodity is a very small percentage of the cost of the final product. Again, the values obtained for the price elasticities of demand for rubber and tin for the 1960s (-0.2 and -0.1, respectively) are typical. Whenever there is an autonomous shift in demand or supply, the low price elasticities of supply and demand will lead to relatively large changes in the export prices and earnings of the exporting countries.

Supply and demand shifts
The supply and demand functions of primary commodities are subject to large and frequent shifts. Changes in the supply can be brought about by at least four categories of factors. First, would be changes in the availability and cost of such inputs as fertilizers, pesticides and water. Second, would be disease, plant exhaustion and production cycles. Third, would be inadequate quality and supply control, warehouse and storage facilities, and farm maintenance practices, and fourth, unexpected changes in government policies. Changes in demand can come about because of changes in the economic conditions in the developed countries and in the world's strategic environment. The changes can be quite marked, especially in the demand for industrial raw materials. Speculation and monopsonistic practices are also important determinants of demand instability.

It is generally accepted that at the global level for different commodities, price instability is more important than volume instability for the majority of the commodities. The explanation for this is that at the global level demand and supply shifts lead mainly to price instability because of the low price elasticity of demand and supply. At the country level, while the price elasticity of supply remains low, that of demand for individual countries, especially small ones, does not. The existence of this crucial difference means that shifts in demand at the country level lead mainly to price instability, while shifts in supply lead mainly to volume instability.

However, there is also support for the contention that at the country level supply factors are, on balance, more important than demand ones in explaining fluctuations in export earnings. The academic studies which provide such support include Glezakos (1973) and Murray (1978). The same point was made by Goreux (1980) in a study for the IMF. More recent evidence is provided by the experience of the IMF-CFF and Stabex schemes. Table 2.1 shows that for the 119 drawings from the IMF-CFF by all of the developing countries over the period 1979-85, volume was more important than price in explaining shortfalls in export earnings in 61 per cent of cases. Supply was more important than demand in explaining the volume shortfall itself in 81 per cent of the cases. Taken together, these figures show that supply was the predominant factor in accounting for shortfalls in export earnings in 50 per cent of the drawings.

The influence of supply factors was even greater in the operation of the Stabex scheme. Table 2.2 shows that volume was more important than price in bringing about shortfalls in export earnings for the period 1975-84, with the exception of 1981. It also shows that natural disasters and adverse production conditions were much more significant than the decline in EC demand in explaining the shortfall in volume itself.

A recent study by UNCTAD (1985) also claims that supply factors are, on balance, more important than demand ones in causing earnings instability at the country level. However, Table 2.3 taken from the UNCTAD study shows that UNCTAD's conclusion holds only when the sample includes countries in which each commodity accounts for between 1 and 5 per cent of a country's total export earnings (i.e. with a threshold of 1 per cent and greater). When the individual commodities account for 5 per cent or more of each country's total export earnings (i.e. threshold of 5 per cent and greater), only 78 of the 170 country/commodity cases show volume instability to be greater than price instability. The opposite result holds for the other 93 cases.

Table 2.1: Frequency in terms of types of cause of export shortfalls in developing countries' drawing on IMF-CFF

(September 1979 - September 1985)

Developing countries by income level [a] (number of drawings)	Causes of earnings shortfall (percentages)		Causes of volume shortfall (percentages)		Predominance of supply in causes of total shortfall
	Volume more important than price	Price more important than volume	Supply more important than demand	Demand more important than supply	
	(1)	(2)	(3)	(4)	(5) = (1) x (3) / 100
I. Below $400 (45)	62	38	86	14	53
II. $500-$1,000 (30)	63	37	84	16	53
III. $1,000-$1,500 (24)	54	46	69	31	37
IV. $1,500-$2,000 (13)	46	54	67	33	31
V. Above $2,000 (7)	86	14	83	17	71
All developing countries (119)	61	39	81	19	50

Source: UNCTAD (1986b), p. 17.

[a] Excludes Hungary, Iceland, Portugal and South Africa.

Table 2.2: Types of cause of export earnings shortfalls in ACP countries' drawing on Stabex, 1975-84

Year of application	Aggregate amount examined	Volume more important than price	Amount of requests attributable to fall in export volume	Breakdown by causes: Natural disasters		Adverse production conditions		Other reasons	
	(m.Ecu[1])	(%)	(m.Ecu)	(m.Ecu)	(%)	(m.Ecu)	(%)	(m.Ecu)	(%)
1975	74.9	100	74.6	22.1	29	23.6	32	28.9	39
1976	28.5	93	26.6	6.5	25	12.8	48	7.3	27
1977	28.8	100	28.8	4.0	14	15.9	55	8.8	31
1978	113.6	98	111.5	74.4	67	28.9	26	8.2	7
1979	57.5	97	56.0	7.0	12	46.4	83	2.6	5
1980	257.7	77	197.4	67.4	34	71.2	36	58.8	30
1981	450.4	35	159.2	42.2	27	71.5	45	45.6	28
1982	106.9	64							
1983	50.5	95							
1984	32.0	93							

Source: UNCTAD (1986b), p. 18.

1 The Ecu is the European Unit of Currency, which was worth US$1.29 in 1975, US$1.39 in 1980 and US$0.73 in 1985.

Table 2.3: Comparison of price instability indices with volume instability indices of exports of primary commodities of developing countries at the country level, 1962-81 [a]

Commodities	Threshold [b]: 1 per cent and greater — Number of countries	1 per cent and greater — Volume instability greater than unit value instability (% of cases)	5 per cent and greater — Number of countries	5 per cent and greater — Volume instability greater than unit value instability (% of cases)
Agricultural				
Groundnuts	7	100	6	100
Groundnut oil	7	88	4	100
Cotton	34	91	21	86
Bovine meat	13	85	7	71
Coconut oil	8	63	4	50
Palm oil	8	63	2	50
Bananas	18	83	11	73
Timber	23	65	12	75
Jute	4	75	2	50
Coffee	36	33	27	11
Sisal	7	43	6	33
Cocoa	23	22	11	9
Sugar	26	27	18	28
Rubber	9	33	6	17
Minerals				
Manganese ore	6	50	-	-
Tin, refined	5	80	3	67
Tin ore	5	80	2	100
Iron ore	14	57	5	60
Copper ore	11	64	6	50
Copper blister	7	57	4	25
Copper, refined	10	40	4	23
Bauxite	6	33	4	40
Phosphate rock	7	14	5	-

Source: UNCTAD (1985), p. 7.

[a] In the case of minerals other countries are included because of their importance in world exports. For some countries adequate data are not available.

[b] Percentage of the commodity's export earnings in total export earnings of the country (average 1976-77).

Taking into account the results of a number of academic studies, the experience of the IMF-CFF and Stabex schemes and, to a lesser extent, the findings of a recent UNCTAD study, there is sufficient evidence for believing that volume instability is more pronounced than price instability at the country level. The implication of this is that, on balance, supply factors are more important than demand factors in explaining instability in export earnings at the country level of analysis. It is also that the policies and mechanisms designed for any stabilization programme should also be able to reduce fluctuations in the supply of primary commodities at the individual commodity and country level.

Commodity and geographical concentration

It may also be important for such a stabilization programme to be aware of the contribution that commodity and geographical concentration can make to instability in export earnings. The tendency towards income instability as a result of supply and, to a lesser extent, demand characteristics may be strengthened by a high degree of commodity and geographical concentration. The dependence on a few commodities will reduce the chances of a country in having fluctuations in one direction in some of its exports being offset by movements in the opposite direction in the other exports. The same risk will be run if the country depends on a few countries for its exports. The basic argument behind the concentration hypothesis is that it is always risky to put all of one's eggs in the same basket.

The empirical support for this plausible-sounding hypothesis is somewhat mixed. From his correlation analysis of the relationship between export instability and export concentration for samples of between sixty-six and seventy-nine countries for 1946-58, Coppock (1962) found correlation coefficients which range from 0.02 to 0.11. An equally weak relationship between the two variables was found by MacBean (1966) in his simple and multiple cross-country regression analyses for roughly the same period. Other cross-country studies which produced no relationship were Massell (1964), Naya (1973), and Brundell, Horn and Svedberg (1981).

As these results go against the conventional wisdom, the studies have been questioned for using unacceptable measures of instability and concentration. However, other studies which use more sophisticated measures of the two variables have also failed to find support for the traditional view. The studies by O'Brien (1972) and Soutar (1977) fall into this category.

It would be fair to say that the number of cross-country studies which show the absence of any positive relationship between export instability and commodity concentration is far greater than the number which show the presence of such a relationship. The study by Michaely (1962) is one of the earliest of the latter category of studies, though the relationship was between price instability and commodity concentration. Massell (1970) did find a positive link between export instability and commodity concentration, but the strength of this relationship became weaker the higher the share of foodstuffs was in the total exports. Other studies which found that a significant proportion of export instability in developing countries was due to commodity concentration are Knudsen and Parnes (1975), Sheedy (1977), and Batchelor, Major and Morgan (1980).

The apparent weakness or absence of any positive relationship between export instability and commodity concentration may be due to three reasons. The first is that export proceeds from individual commodities tend to move in the same direction. The second is that countries with high commodity concentration tend to specialize in relatively stable commodities. The third is that the instability indices of a country's export commodities vary very markedly (MacBean and Nguyen, 1980; Turner and Lambert, 1981).

These factors have been used very effectively by Love (1979) to explain why cross-country studies cannot adequately capture any causal relationship that might exist between export instability and commodity concentration. When time-series analysis at the country level is carried out with properly defined explanatory variables, commodity concentration was found to have contributed to earnings instability for a larger number of developing countries.

There are fewer studies on the relationship between export instability and geographical concentration. But these also do not provide clear-cut results. Coppock (1962) and Massell (1964) produced results which do not support the hypothesized positive relationship. The relationship produced was, in fact, a negative one but this was not statistically significant. A negative but insignificant relationship was also obtained by MacBean (1966) in his simple correlation analysis. However, when multiple regression analysis was used, he found that geographical concentration was negatively and significantly correlated with export instability. A more recent study by Brundell, Horn and Svedberg (1981), shows that geographical concentration had no influence at all on export instability for a large group of developing countries for 1965-77.

Other factors
Besides supply and demand factors and commodity and geographical concentration, it is possible to identify other quite different causes of export instability. One may be the size of a country: a smaller country has a narrower range of natural resources and therefore less flexibility to deal with internal and external economic disturbances (Erb and Schiavo-Campo, 1969). Another may be the level of development of a country: a more advanced country produces more of relatively finished products, which are more stable, and has a more flexible and sophisticated production base. However, the number of empirical studies to back these claims is very small.

Conclusions

Three unambiguous conclusions can be drawn from the discussion so far. The first is that those resource-rich developing countries with a large export sector that is dominated by a few primary commodities have a high level of export instability. The second is that the supply and demand conditions prevailing in the primary commodity sector are an important cause of this fluctuation. The role of commodity and geographical concentration in export instability is less clear-cut, though the weight of the evidence suggests that it is not as important as commonly believed. The third is that supply factors are more important than demand factors in destabilizing export earnings at the country level. Does this supply-induced export instability slow down economic growth? This is the topic of the next chapter.

3
Export Instability and Economic Growth

Transmission of Export Instability

The hypothesis that export instability affects the growth of primary-producing developing countries adversely consists of three distinct but related parts (Lim, 1976). The first is that the developing countries have a high degree of export instability. This has just been demonstrated to be the case, with the source of the instability coming from both the supply and demand sides, but with supply factors being generally more important at the country level. The second is that export instability is transmitted to the rest of the economy, and the third that the resultant economic instability is harmful to the growth of the economy.

While the nature and the causes of export instability have been examined extensively in the theoretical and empirical literature, the same cannot be said of the second part of the hypothesis of the adverse effect of export instability on economic growth, that instability in the export sector has been transmitted to the rest of the economy. In fact, it has been largely neglected in the cross-country and time-series studies. It is difficult to know why most of the studies assume that export instability will automatically lead to economic instability, and bring with it the factors which hinder economic growth (Wilson, 1983).

A change in the export proceeds of a developing country will affect its economy through the direct effect on the incomes of the producers in the export sector and through the indirect multiplier and accelerator effects. These will produce changes in the gross national product (GNP) which move in the same direction and which, in the absence of any government intervention and leakages, will be more than proportional to the initial changes in the export earnings.

This is the gist of the theory and the empirical verification of it should consist of two steps. The first is to show that changes in the GNP and export proceeds move consistently in the same direction and the second is to calculate the foreign-trade multiplier in order to know the size of the effect of export instability on the rest of the economy.

There are thus no conceptual difficulties in establishing the relationship between export instability and economic instability. However, the empirical verification of it has left much to be desired. First, there is an unfortunate tendency to measure the impact of export instability on the gross domestic product (GDP) and not the GNP. The former includes profits repatriated overseas and if foreign ownership is significant and foreign companies allow such profits to fluctuate while keeping their operating costs and payments to the host country steady, the use of the GDP will exaggerate the degree of economic instability created, even if the correct foreign-trade multiplier is used. Second, many studies have tried to establish the relationship between changes in the GNP and changes in the export earnings with the use of time-series which are far too short for meaningful relationships to be established.

Even if the above weaknesses are absent, there is the further problem that most studies have analysed the transmission process at too aggregated a level. Typically there is little interest in the specific channels through which instability in export earnings is transmitted to the rest of the economy. Not only does this approach ignore the underlying structural relationships between export earnings and the rest of the economy, it also produces results which have only limited use to policy-makers as it cannot identify the variables that they can act on.

A recent study (Lim, 1981) goes some way in remedying this weakness by (i) examining the effects of export instability on government revenue and on the various sub-categories of this revenue and (ii) estimating the contribution of the various sub-categories of revenue to the instability of the total government revenue, for a sample of forty-five developing countries over the period 1965-73. Government revenue is chosen as the intermediary as it is made up of personal and corporate income taxes, sales taxes, customs duties (export and import taxes), other taxes (e.g. property taxes), and non-tax revenue (e.g. profits of government-owned enterprises). As long as fluctuations in export earnings result in fluctuations in domestic incomes, income taxes, other taxes and non-tax revenue will be affected. The same can be said of the demand for domestically produced and imported goods and so the amount of sales taxes and import duties collected.

In order to test for the effects of export instability on revenue instability, the following two equations were estimated by ordinary least-squares, for the sample of forty-five developing countries. Linear functions were also used, but logarithmic ones produced, in general, better results.

$$\log \dot{TGR} = \log a_1 + b_1 \log \dot{X} \qquad (3.1)$$

$$\log \dot{GTR} = \log a_2 + b_2 \log \dot{X} \qquad (3.2)$$

$\dot{TGR}$, $\dot{GTR}$ and $\dot{X}$ are the instability indices for total government revenue (TGR), government tax revenue (GTR) and export earnings (X) respectively, for the period 1965-73. They are represented by the standard errors of estimate obtained by regressing TGR, GTR and X respectively on time over the period 1965-73. The results are:

$$\log \dot{TGR} = \underset{(2.067)^{**}}{1.581} + \underset{(3.718)^{*}}{0.635} \log \dot{X} \qquad (3.3)$$

$$\bar{R}^2 = 0.225 \qquad \text{F-ratio} = 13.761^{*}$$

$$\log \dot{GTR} = \underset{(2.178)^{**}}{1.555} + \underset{(3.317)^{*}}{0.559} \log \dot{X} \qquad (3.4)$$

$$\bar{R}^2 = 0.185 \qquad \text{F-ratio} = 11.006^{*}$$

The figures in parentheses are t values, while * and ** indicate statistical significance at the 1 and the 5 per cent levels of significance respectively. The values of the adjusted coefficient of determination ($\bar{R}^2$) show that factors other than export instability were more important in "explaining" government revenue instability. They also suggest that the multiplier and the accelerator effects are not as important as generally believed, or that counter-cyclical fiscal and monetary policies have been successfully implemented to cushion the domestic economy from export fluctuations, or that random factors have been operating consistently to offset variations in export earnings (e.g. the harvesting of a bumper rice crop which compensates for a drop in export proceeds from rubber).

We can ignore the effects of counter-cyclical measures and random happenings. The former would require a sophistication in fiscal and monetary management that is not possible even in the most advanced country, while the latter is improbable. This leaves only the smallness of the multiplier and the accelerator effects as a possible reason for the insensitivity of the domestic sector to export fluctuations.

When domestic investments and government expenditures are assumed to be constant and foreign repercussions ignored, the foreign-trade multiplier is given by:

$$1 / (m + s + t) \tag{3.5}$$

where m, s and t are the marginal propensities to import, save and tax respectively. MacBean (1966) has correctly pointed out that this conventional measure should be adjusted to take into account, among other things, repatriated profits by foreign firms and the import content of exports. Accordingly, a more appropriate measure of the foreign-trade multiplier will be:

$$(1 - p_x - m_x) / (m + s + t) \tag{3.6}$$

where p_x is the proportion of export earnings repatriated, and m_x the proportion of export earnings accounted by imports for re-exports.

The unweighted averages of p_x, m_x, m, s and t for the forty-five countries are 0.11, 0.05, 0.31, 0.23 and 0.14 respectively. The unweighted averages of the unadjusted and the adjusted foreign-trade multipliers worked out to be 1.47 and 1.23 respectively. These values show that the secondary repercussion of a change in export earnings was relatively small. They are consistent with the result that export instability was not an important determinant of government revenue instability: if fluctuations in export earnings are transmitted only weakly to the rest of the economy, then fluctuations in government revenue are also likely to be little affected by the export instability.

It is generally believed that the restrictive assumptions of the accelerator theory make its operation either very weak or non-existent. We do not have the statistical data for our sample to test for the significance of the accelerator effect. However, whatever data we have suggests that none of the central assumptions of the accelerator model is valid. Thus recent empirical studies show that capital stock is grossly underutilized in developing countries so that the assumption that there is no excess capacity does not hold (Phan-Thuy, Betancourt, Winston and Kabaj, 1981; Bautista, Hughes, Lim, Morawetz and Thoumi, 1981). Nor does the available evidence support the assumptions that capital and output are forever related in a fixed ratio and that every change in income creates an expectation that income will remain high.

The combination of a weak multiplier effect and a weak or non-existent accelerator effect may explain much of the insensitivity of

ROUTLEDGE
11 New Fetter Lane
London EC4P 4EE
Telephone: 071-583 9855
Fax: 071-583 4519

SDS

We have much pleasure in sending you the accompanying book for review

Title: Export Instability & Compensatory Financing

Author: Lim

ISBN: Hb 0 415 03645 3
Pb

Publication Date: 3.1.91

Published Price: £ 35.00 Hb

£ Pb

A copy of the review would be greatly appreciated. Reviews should not appear in the press prior to the date of publication.
For further information please contact:

James Wilson

domestic incomes and government revenues to fluctuations in the export sector for our sample of developing countries over the period 1965-73. However, it should be pointed out that the experiences of individual countries with large foreign and entrepôt activities may be quite different. In the case, for example, of Malaysia, the value of the foreign trade multiplier would have been reduced from 1.33 to 0.80 (Lim, 1974).

The effect of export instability on revenue instability, though small, cannot be ignored and it would be useful to identify the specific channels through which export instability was transmitted to the government revenue sector. Total government revenue is made up of personal and corporate income taxes (INT), sales taxes (SAT), customs duties (CUD), other taxes (OTT), and non-tax revenue (NTR) as, for example, the profits of government-owned or government-run enterprises. OTT consists of excize taxes, stamp duties and so on. The sum of INT, SAT, CUD and OTT is, of course, equal to GTR. In order to find out which sources of revenue acted as transmission channels, the following equations were estimated for the sample of forty-five developing countries.

$$\log \dot{INT} = \log a_3 + b_3 \log \dot{X} \qquad (3.7)$$

$$\log \dot{SAT} = \log a_4 + b_4 \log \dot{X} \qquad (3.8)$$

$$\log \dot{CUD} = \log a_5 + b_5 \log \dot{X} \qquad (3.9)$$

$$\log \dot{OTT} = \log a_6 + b_6 \log \dot{X} \qquad (3.10)$$

$$\log \dot{NTR} = \log a_7 + b_7 \log \dot{X} \qquad (3.11)$$

$\dot{INT}$, $\dot{SAT}$, $\dot{CUD}$, $\dot{OTT}$ and $\dot{NTR}$ are the instability indices for income taxes, sales taxes, customs duties, other taxes and non-tax revenue, and were calculated by the same method as used for estimating $\dot{TGR}$, $\dot{GTR}$ and $\dot{X}$.

The results, given in Table 3.1, show that export instability was channelled to the government revenue sector through the collections of non-tax revenue, income taxes, sales taxes and other taxes, in descending order of importance. The relative importance of these four sources of revenue is consistent with what is known about the forms in which these revenues are collected in most developing countries. Thus, as non-tax revenue includes such items as the profits of public utilities and government-run enterprises it will vary directly with fluctuations in the domestic economy. Income taxes are levied on a progressive and flat *ad valorem* basis so that instability in their collection is closely related to instability in the domestic economy. This relationship is often weakened by the shortage of skilled and honest tax personnel, so that the link may not be as strong as that between non-tax revenue instability and export instability. Sales taxes and other taxes are collected on an *ad valorem* and a specific basis, with specific taxes, whose revenue tends to fluctuate less with fluctuations in the domestic economy, being more prevalent in the collection of other taxes (Due, 1970).

Table 3.1: Cross-country logarithmic regressions explaining instability of sub-categories of total government revenue: forty-five developing countries, 1965–73

	Dependent variables				
Independent variables	$IN\dot{T}$	$SA\dot{T}$	$C\dot{U}D$	$O\dot{T}T$	$N\dot{I}R$
Constant	0.416	0.252	2.753	-0.607	0.354
	(0.566)	(0.287)	(2.494)**	(-0.532)	(0.461)
$\dot{X}$	0.584	0.544	-0.088	0.574	0.679
	(3.366)*	(2.627)**	(-0.338)	(2.134)**	(3.746)*
$\bar{R}^2$	0.190	0.118	-0.021	0.075	0.229
F-ratio	11.328*	6.900**	0.114	4.556**	14.035

* and ** denote statistical significance at the 1 and 5 per cent levels of significance respectively.

The collection of customs duties did not fluctuate in line with fluctuations in export earnings because import duties, unlike export taxes, are usually collected in arrears. An export boom, which follows an export slump, will lead to an increase in the revenue from export taxes. However, the revenue from import duties, which are collected with a one-year lag, will be low and therefore will offset the increase in the revenue from export taxes.

How much did instability in each of the sub-categories of revenue, caused mainly by factors other than export instability, contribute to the instability of the total government revenue and the instability of the government tax revenue? Clearly, the contribution of a sub-category of revenue to the instability of, for example, total government revenue depends on: (i) the degree of instability of the sub-category of revenue and (ii) the share of the sub-category of revenue in the total government revenue. The sub-category may be very unstable, but if it is a relatively minor sub-category then its contribution to the instability of the total government revenue will be relatively small.

Mathematically, the contribution of the jth sub-category (C_j) to the instability of the total government revenue is given by:

$$C_j = \left(I_j \bar{R}_j\right) / \left(\sum_{j=1}^{k} I_j \bar{R}_j\right) \qquad (3.12)$$

where I_j is the instability index of the jth sub-category of revenue, k the number of sub-categories and $\bar{R}_j$ the arithmetic mean of the jth sub-category over the period under analysis. This formula is taken from Idachaba (1975:103) which is, in turn, a variant of an index first introduced by Coppock (1962).

We calculated (i) the relative contributions of government tax revenue (GTR) and non-tax revenue (NTR) to the instability of total government revenue (TGR), and (ii) the relative contributions of income taxes (INT), sales taxes (SAT), customs duties (CUD) and other taxes (OTT) to the instability of government tax revenue (GTR), for each of the forty-five countries over the period 1965-73. Table 3.2 presents the unweighted averages of C_j for the sample of forty-five countries. It also gives the unweighted averages of the shares of the various sub-categories in TGR and GTR (S_j). This is given by $R_j / \sum_{j=1}^{k} R_j$ where k is the number of sub-categories and R_j the revenue of the jth sub-category.

It can be seen that instability in government tax revenue (GTR) was much more important than instability in non-tax revenue (NTR) in contributing to the instability of total government revenue (TGR). This dominance of GTR was due not only to its greater importance in the TGR (78.6% as against 21.4% for NTR), but also to its greater instability (304.3 as against 173.6 for NTR).

Given the overriding importance of the contributions of GTR to the instability of TGR, it is important to know the relative importance of the contributions of the sub-categories of GTR to the instability of the GTR itself. The results, given in Table 3.2, show that the biggest contribution came from customs duties (CUD), with a share of 34.9%, followed by income taxes (INT, 28.4%), sales taxes (SAT, 24.9%) and other taxes (OTT, 11.8%). The table also shows that the values of C_j and S_j for the four sub-categories of government tax revenue are not statistically different from each other, to suggest that the four sub-categories experienced approximately the same degree of instability.

Table 3.2: Contributions of revenue sub-categories to instability of total government revenue and government tax revenue (C_j) and shares of revenue sub-categories in total government revenue and government tax revenue (S_j)

	C_j	S_j	$(C_j-S_j)^1$
Instability in total government revenue (TGR):	100.0	100.0	
Government tax revenue (GTR)	83.7	78.6	s.s.
Non-tax revenue (NTR)	16.3	21.4	s.s.
Instability in government tax revenue (GTR):	100.0	100.0	
Income Taxes (INT)	28.4	27.9	s.i.
Sales taxes (SAT)	24.9	27.0	s.i.
Customs duties (CUD)	34.9	31.7	s.i.
Other taxes (OTT)	11.8	13.4	s.i.

1 s.s. = statistically significant at the 5 per cent level of confidence.
s.i. = statistically insignificant at the 5 per cent level of confidence.

The analysis so far has produced three main findings. The most important is that export instability had only a relatively small influence on the domestic incomes and government revenues of the sample of forty-five countries over the period 1965-73. The popular belief in the existence of sizeable multiplier and accelerator effects is not warranted because of the presence of two significant groups of leakages. First, there are the traditional and well-known leakages of imports, savings and taxes. Second, there are the less well-known leakages of the repatriation of profits and the import content of export earnings. Both groups of leakages had helped to moderate the internal impact of export instability.

The second finding of interest is that whatever instability was transmitted from the export sector to the rest of the economy was done through the collection of non-tax revenue, income taxes, sales taxes and excize taxes, in descending order of importance. The collection of export and import duties did not act as a transmission channel.

The third finding is that the main source of instability in government revenue was the tax revenue sector, while the main source of instability in the tax revenue itself was the customs duties sector.

The next stage in the analysis is to examine the relationship between instability in government revenue and instability in government expenditure. The governments of most developing countries depend basically on their tax and non-tax revenues to finance their expenditure programmes. Unless countervailing action is taken, instability in government revenue will result in instability in government expenditure.

In Lim (1983), instability indices were calculated for total government revenue, total government expenditure and the various sub-categories of government expenditure for each of the forty-five countries. The median values of these indices for the total, African, Western Hemisphere and Asian samples of countries are given in Table 3.3.

For the African sample, government revenue fluctuated considerably more than total government expenditure. For the Asian sample, the difference was not so marked, while for the Western Hemisphere one there was no difference at all. For the total sample, revenue instability exceeded expenditure instability quite significantly. This suggests that for developing countries as a whole, certain factors had operated to soften the destabilizing effect of revenue instability.

Table 3.3: Median instability indices of government revenue, expenditure and expenditure sub-categories, 1965-73

	Total (45)	Africa (21)	Western Hemisphere (13)	Asia (11)
Government Revenue	64	54	25	126
Government Expenditure	48	20	25	112
Agriculture	6	4	2	12
Education	6	3	4	13
Health	3	2	2	8
Transport	7	5	5	23
Defence	13	7	5	34
Industry	5	5	1	17
Other	29	15	11	62

The postulated positive relationship between revenue instability ($\dot{R}$) and expenditure instability ($\dot{E}$) is given by ST in Figure 3.1a. Other things being equal, an increase in $\dot{R}$, from OB_1 to OB_2 will produce an increase in $\dot{E}$ from OC_1 to OC_2.

One of the factors which may weaken or even invalidate this relationship is the availability of international reserves. Given the overriding aim of maintaining expenditure stability, a government of a developing country with an abundant supply of such reserves can cushion the impact of revenue instability by drawing on these reserves.

In Figure 3.1b the actual international reserves to imports ratio is given by the ray OA, while the desired ratio is given by the ray OD. The increase in expenditure instability, from OC_1 to OC_2 in Figure 3.1a, as a result of the increase in revenue instability from OB_1 to OB_2, can be avoided if the government were to reduce its reserves to imports ratio from ray OA to ray OD. For a given imports level, OM_1, this will mean running down the reserves from OI_1 to OI_2. International reserves can thus act as a buffer mechanism and produce an effect equivalent to the shifting of ST to S'T'. Thus, the higher IR is the more it enables the government to reduce its expenditure instability for a given level of revenue instability.

Figure 3.1: Cushioning effect of international reserves

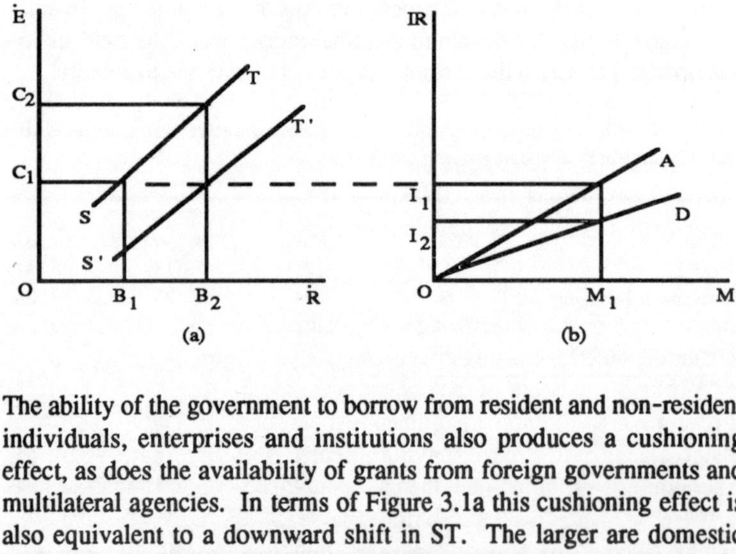

The ability of the government to borrow from resident and non-resident individuals, enterprises and institutions also produces a cushioning effect, as does the availability of grants from foreign governments and multilateral agencies. In terms of Figure 3.1a this cushioning effect is also equivalent to a downward shift in ST. The larger are domestic borrowing, foreign borrowing and the amount of grants received, the easier it is for the government to reduce fluctuations in its expenditure for a given level of fluctuation in its revenue.

The following estimating equation was therefore used to identify the determinants of expenditure instability:

$$\dot{E} = f(\dot{R}, IR, DB, FB, FG) \qquad (3.13)$$

$\dot{E}$ and $\dot{R}$ are the instability indices for government expenditure and revenue respectively, for the period 1965-73. IR is the average of the developing country's holdings of gold, Special Drawing Rights and foreign exchange as a percentage of its imports of goods and non-factor services over the period 1965-73. DB, FB and FG are the averages of domestic borrowing, foreign borrowing and foreign grants respectively, as a percentage of government expenditure over the same period. $\dot{R}$ is expected to be positively related to $\dot{E}$, while IR, DB, FB and FG are expected to be negatively related to $\dot{E}$.

Equation (3.13) was estimated in its linear and logarithmic formulations, with intercepts, by ordinary least squares. The logarithmic function produces the better result, which is given by:

$$\log \dot{E} = \underset{(1.833)^c}{0.469} + \underset{(405.613)^a}{0.915} \log \dot{R} - \underset{(-4.614)^a}{0.081} \log IR$$

$$- \underset{(-32.191)^a}{0.169} \log DB - \underset{(-38.776)^a}{0.217} \log FB - \underset{(-5.510)^a}{0.004} \log FG$$

$$\bar{R}^2 = 0.899 \qquad \text{F-ratio} = 79.162^b \qquad (3.14)$$

The figures in parentheses are the t values while a, b and c indicate their statistical significance at the 0.0005, 0.01 and 0.05 levels of confidence respectively. The results show that government revenue instability was the most important 'cause' of government expenditure instability. However, they also show that the availability of international reserves, domestic and foreign borrowing and foreign grants had played a part in dampening the destabilizing effects of revenue fluctuations.

Though a number of factors had softened the destabilizing effects of revenue instability on government expenditure, the latter is still very unstable. If the aim of having greater stability in government expenditure is still important, then a second line of defence may have to be used. This is to identify, first, the sectoral sources of spending instability and, second, the actions that can be taken to reduce instability within such sectors.

The contribution that the jth sub-category (C_j) makes to the instability of, say, total government expenditure is given by:

$$C_j = 100\left(I_j \bar{E}_j\right) / \left(C \sum_{j=1}^{k} I_j \bar{E}_j\right) \qquad (3.15)$$

where I_j is the instability index of the jth sub-category of expenditure, k the number of sub-categories and $\bar{E}_j$ the arithmetic mean of the jth sub-category over the period under analysis.

For each of the forty-five countries over the period 1965-73, we calculated C_j of the various sectors in the instability of total government expenditure, government development expenditure and government recurrent expenditure. The unweighted averages of C_j, I_j and $\bar{E}_j$ for the sample of forty-five countries are given in Table 3.4.

The relative sizes of the sectoral total expenditures are in line with results of previous studies on the subject. These figures must, of course, be interpreted with care in view of the size of the 'other' sector which was obtained as the residual sector. Inter-sectoral comparisons were made without reference to the 'other' sector. The largest share went into education. This was followed by the defence sector, a finding of considerable interest in view of the finding that defence spending has detrimental effects on economic growth. The relatively small share going to agriculture shows the traditional neglect of what is usually the largest sector in the economies of developing countries.

The main sources of total expenditure instability were the defence, education and transport sectors. The importance of these sectors was due both to their high degree of instability (high I_js) and to their dominating share of government expenditure (high E_js). For the transport sector, the instability in spending stemmed from the development side. This had to do with the fact that transport expenditure comes in big lumps. For educational expenditure, the instability originated largely from the recurrent side. This might have reflected the unfortunately widespread tendency to treat recurrent spending as consumption and development spending as investment. Recurrent and development expenditures on defence were unfortunately presented together so it is not possible to identify the main source of spending fluctuation. The instability of defence spending as a whole was probably due to the lumpiness of defence spending and the tendency for such expenditure to vary according to the frequent changes in internal and external political events.

It would thus seem that the scope for reducing overall spending instability by reducing sectoral spending instability is rather limited as it is confined to reducing instability in recurrent educational spending. A number of factors have accounted for this ineffectiveness. First, the sectors with the most stable spending (agriculture and health) were minor recipients of government funds. As the allocation of government funds among competing claims is guided by historical and economic factors which cannot be changed in the short run, the room for countervailing action here is small. Second, expenditure in those sectors which have been favoured (transport and defence) comes in big lumps. This lumpiness is technologically determined and the possibility of reducing it is rather small. Third, the internal and external political factors which make for fluctuating defence spending are largely outside the control of economic policy-makers in developing countries.

Table 3.4: Composition of government expenditure instability in forty-five developing Countries, 1965-73

	I_j	$\bar{E}_j$	C_j
Total government expenditure	304	100.0	100.0
Agriculture	28	6.9	3.0
Education	68	16.4	8.9
Health	23	6.5	1.7
Transport	43	8.6	6.6
Defence	90	12.9	10.8
Industry	58	2.6	2.6
Other	721	46.1	66.4
Government development expenditure	237	100.0	100.0
Agriculture	37	15.1	9.6
Education	22	6.4	2.4
Health	18	3.1	1.1
Transport	63	23.3	22.8
Industry	58	12.2	12.3
Other	129	39.9	51.8
Government recurrent expenditure	323	100.0	100.0
Agriculture	20	4.5	1.3
Education	72	19.1	10.6
Health	24	7.3	1.9
Transport	16	4.7	2.3
Defence	90	16.3	13.7
Other	843	48.1	70.2

The analysis shows that the reduction of sectoral spending instability *per se* and the use of international reserves and various forms of borrowing and aid can only have a peripheral effect in decreasing the instability of overall government spending. It suggests that efforts need to be concentrated on reducing the degree of revenue instability, as revenue instability was the main 'cause' of spending instability. It is important to identify the channels through which export fluctuations have been transmitted to the rest of the economy, as this would help government policy-makers to increase the automaticity of the counter-cyclical machinery and therefore to reduce the opportunity cost.

A Priori Arguments Against Instability

For those resource-rich developing countries with a concentrated and large export sector whose instability is transmitted to the rest of the economy, the issues of the adverse impact of economic instability on economic welfare and growth become important. The first issue, that of the impact of instability on welfare, is a static one and is non-controversial. The second issue, that of the impact of instability on growth, is a dynamic and a controversial one and has received a great deal of attention in the development literature.

If export instability is caused by a shift in demand, the producers of the commodities concerned will not benefit from having greater stability because of the lower producer surplus generated, while the consumers will gain. The world community will benefit from greater stability and the producers will only benefit if some of the consumers' gain can be channelled to them. If the instability is caused by a shift in supply, the reverse results hold: the producers gain and the consumers lose from having greater stability. However, the world as a whole would gain and the producers will only persuade the consumers to join a commodity stabilizing scheme if some of the producers' gain can be passed on to the consumers (Lindert and Kindleberger, 1982: Appendix F).

These are the static concerns of the discussion of the effect of export instability on the economy and are considered to be much less important than the dynamic concerns. Certainly the whole debate on the relationship between export instability and economic growth pays scant attention to them.

The arguments that have been put forward for believing that export instability is detrimental to economic growth are usually presented at three levels. A careful examination of these and the empirical support for them is needed in order to see whether the existing compensatory financing facilities have been designed to cope with the entire range of economic ills arising from export instability.

The first set of arguments emphasizes the adverse effects that instability has on investment. An autonomous increase in export proceeds generates increased incomes in the export sector which in turn may lead to higher wages and government expenditures. A subsequent fall in export earnings may not produce a proportionate decrease in labour costs and government expenditures as these are rather sticky in the downward direction for political, social and economic reasons. There is a tendency to deal with this "ratchet effect" by drawing upon the gold and foreign exchange reserves, and, when this avenue is exhausted, by imposing import quotas. The effect of this is to shift demand to domestically produced goods and, unless the production of such goods can respond adequately, this will probably lead to a rise in the cost of living. This may well act as the starting point for another round of wage increases.

Investment under inflationary conditions usually ends in real estate and the purchase of land, and not in private or public projects which have long gestation periods. While the total investment level in the short run might not be affected, the types of investment activities encouraged by a speculative mentality are not those required for sustained economic growth. In the long run the total level of investment will be lowered.

Export instability may also reduce investment through the precautionary discounting of potential investment returns. Public and private investment programmes complement each other to a large extent. If export instability produces instability in public expenditure, this may reduce the confidence that private investors have in the ability of the government to provide the necessary complementary public facilities and so discourage private investment.

Another way in which export instability can reduce investment is by increasing the cost of investment through either business miscalculations or the extra costs incurred by hedging against uncertainty. The lack of information and of a sophisticated capital and futures market would make such increases in costs prohibitive.

The second set of arguments against export instability centres around the administrative problems it can create for governments. The recurrent balance-of-payments crises and the constant need to impose import controls on consumption goods to preserve scarce foreign exchange, as a result of a multitude of uncertainties in the development process, will divert the attention of scarce government personnel from other important development functions. The import of strategic intermediate and capital goods at crucial moments in the implementation of development plans can also be impeded. Greater economic uncertainty may also force governments to hold larger international reserves and reduce their already low capacity to import important goods. Export instability can contribute to this general level of uncertainty. To the extent that it does so significantly, export instability can affect the planning and growth processes adversely.

The third argument is the more general one that export instability, together with other sources of uncertainty in the economy (e.g. instability in crop production and foreign aid receipts) can bring about social and political instability. Uncertainty in the prices and incomes that people already in abject poverty receive can further increase their dissatisfaction and lead to social and even political unrest. One important effect of this may be a slowing down of the rate of economic growth.

Results of Empirical Studies

Three different approaches have been used to test for the effects of export instability on economic growth. The most popular is the cross-country regression analysis which attempts to sum up the experiences of a large sample of developing countries over a given, and rather short, period (e.g. Glezakos, 1973). When long and reliable time-series data on individual countries are available, the country-study approach is used (e.g. Ariff, 1972). Then there is the formal statistical modelling approach, with the use of either a general model to explain growth in a group of countries or a different model for each country (e.g. Priovolos, 1981).

A large number of empirical studies have been carried out and they can be divided, in terms of results, into three groups. The first consists of studies which show export instability to have slowed down the rate of economic growth or of the growth rate of some of its determinants. Prominent in this category are the cross-country studies by Maizels (1968), Glezakos (1973), Lim (1976), Moran (1983), Guillaumont (1987) and Love (1989).

The second group consists of those studies which show instability to have no impact on growth. They include the cross-country studies of MacBean (1966), Voivodas (1974) and Massell (1964), the case studies by Reynolds (1963) on Chile and Ariff (1972) on Malaysia, and some of the econometric modelling work on Zambia, Brazil and the Ivory Coast (Adams and Behrman, 1982).

Then there are the studies which show instability to have stimulated either economic growth or some of its determinants. They include the cross-country studies by Knudsen and Parnes (1975) and Knudsen and Yotopoulos (1976). The *a priori* argument here is that a higher level of export instability would tend to produce a lower propensity to consume out of permanent income because higher reserves are needed to maintain permanent consumption during shortfalls in income. This adaption of Friedman's permanent income hypothesis of consumption would then see instability as leading to a higher level of savings and economic growth. Another argument, put forward by Caine (1954) in his early case study of the then Malaya, is that export instability produces a "ratchet effect" on investment. An export boom-induced investment may not be matched by disinvestment in a period of export slump. The heavy capital expenditure and the large expected future income stream will not only make disinvestment impractical but will also exert constant pressure to reduce the cost of production whenever there is a fall in export prices.

Hirschman (1958) also suggested that instability could be good for growth. Investment may be increased when import-substituting activities are encouraged by the drop in foreign exchange and the rise in import restrictions subsequent to the export shortfalls.

It is clear even from this brief survey of the empirical literature that the picture is a very confused one (Love, 1987). There are inconsistencies in the results obtained by the cross-sectional studies themselves, as there are among the results of the case studies and of the modelling studies. It is also not possible to discern any pattern in the results obtained between the three types of studies.

A number of serious weaknesses in all of the three types of studies may have been responsible for producing such conflicting results.

Inappropriate choice of countries

The first is the failure to recognize that the issue of export instability and economic growth is only important for special types of developing countries. These are countries with important export sectors which are dominated by a few primary products. Thus the developing countries selected for inclusion in cross-country studies or for case studies should only be those with large export sectors and a high degree of commodity concentration. Those not so characterized cannot be affected by instability in the ways postulated by theory and should, therefore, not be included in any study. The exercise is different in kind from those cross-sectional studies which attempt to identify and establish universal patterns of behaviour and change and which, therefore, require as comprehensive a sample as possible. It would be an unsatisfactory procedure to refer to such official international publications as the World Bank's *World Tables* or the International Monetary Fund's *International Financial Statistics* and include all those developing countries for which data on certain predetermined variables are available.

The lack of criteria for the selection of countries for study may also leave room for bias, if, for example, certain countries were left out deliberately on some pretext because their inclusion would have produced results that were not expected. Possible criteria are to include only those with above-average export shares and commodity concentrations. The use of such criteria can, of course, be criticized but it does have the advantage of introducing an element of consistency in the selection procedure.

Most of the cross-sectional studies have not been careful enough in their choice of countries. MacBean (1966) and Ariff (1972), two of the earliest cross-sectional studies, have basically the same sample of developing countries but did not say what their selection criteria were. The sample used by Kenen and Voivodas (1972) was different but no reason was given for the divergence, while a latter study by Voivodas (1974) did not even list the countries included.

A good example of the few studies which have been careful in the choice of countries is the work of Glezakos (1973). He was very critical of those studies which included countries "which, according to *a priori* arguments, are not significantly affected by export instability" (Glezakos, 1973:672). Glezakos was interested in testing the effect of export instability on import capacity and so included in his sample only those countries whose import capacity depended on their export proceeds. Such countries as Taiwan and Mauritius were excluded as foreign aid and tourism played an important role in financing their investment programmes. In view of the entirely different result obtained by Maizels (1968), when he re-estimated the relationship between export instability and economic growth, using basically the same function as MacBean (1966) but with a more discriminate use of the data, the need for choosing an appropriate sample of developing countries is clear.

Given that different cross-sectional studies have looked at different groups of developing countries selected on different principles, it is really not surprising that the results of such studies can produce such conflicting results. Some country-studies have tested the instability hypothesis for countries which clearly, on a *prima facie* basis, cannot be affected by instability. For such studies, failure to capture any relationship between export instability and economic growth does not mean that there is no link between the two variables for developing countries as a whole.

Inadequate structural formulations

Another important weakness of most of the existing studies is the failure to derive their estimating equations systematically in ways that are consistent with the hypotheses they are supposed to be testing. The mis-specification of the relationships can produce results which have no bearing or relevance to the debate.

Take the case of the very influential study by MacBean (1966). The following basic estimating equations were used:

$$Y_g = f(\dot{X}, MC, TR) \tag{3.16}$$

$$I_g = f(\dot{X}, MC, F) \tag{3.17}$$

$$I_g = f(\dot{X}, MC, F, MK_1, MK_2) \tag{3.18}$$

$$I_g = f(\dot{X}, MC, MK_1, MK_2) \tag{3.19}$$

where Y_g is the growth rate of the real GDP, I_g the growth rate of real investment, I/Y the investment to GDP ratio, $\dot{X}$ export instability, MC the growth rate of the total import capacity, T the foreign trade to GDP ratio, R the change in gold and foreign exchange reserves, F the growth rate of foreign exchange reserves, MK_1 the capital goods imports to the domestic fixed capital formation ratio and MK_2 the capital goods imports to the total imports ratio.

No explanation was given for the choice of the determinants other than $\dot{X}$ and for the different combinations of them. Nor was there any indication as to which version of the general hypothesis was being tested. It would appear from the emphasis given to import-oriented variables that MacBean was testing the hypothesis that instability disrupts the import of important intermediate and capital goods and so hinders economic growth. Yet if the logic of that particular argument were to be followed, then equations 3.18 and 3.19 are mis-specified. The effect of export instability is to make imported intermediate and capital goods unavailable at crucial moments in the development process, so that $\dot{X}$ acts on I_g and I/Y through its influence on MK_1 or MK_2. As such, $\dot{X}$ and MK_1 or MK_2 should not appear as determinants in the same estimating equation.

The proper procedure is to begin making I_g a positive function of MK, which is the imports of capital goods expressed as a proportion of either domestic fixed capital formation or the total import bill. This relationship is postulated because of the technical and economic complementarity between locally produced and foreign produced capital goods. If MC and F are also included as determinants of I_g, then the investment function can be written as $I_g = f$ (MK, MC, F). The MK function should then be presented as MK = $f(\dot{X})$ and the substitution of this into the I_g function would yield an estimating equation which is similar to equation 3.17, and different from equation 3.18, in not having $\dot{X}$ and MK in the same estimating equation. If the same procedure was adopted in deriving the investment ratio (I/Y) function, then equation 3.18 would have to be presented as I/Y = f ($\dot{X}$, MC).

The same type of criticism can be made of the estimating equations used by Kenen and Voivodas (1972), which were:

$$Y_g = f(\dot{X}, AR, P_g, I/Y, A) \qquad (3.20)$$

$$I_g = f(\dot{X}, AR, P_g, A) \qquad (3.21)$$

$$I/Y = f(\dot{X}, AR, P_g) \qquad (3.22)$$

$\dot{X}$, the instability index, is the standard error of a regression trend line, obtained by a first-order auto-regressive scheme, divided by the mean of the export proceeds, and AR is the auto-regressive coefficient of the trend line. P_g is the inflation rate and the other variables are as defined previously.

Again no derivational procedure for the estimating equations was given. However, it would appear from the inclusion of P_g in all of the three equations and the inclusion of I/Y in equation 3.20 that the inflationary argument against instability was being tested. If this is indeed the case, the equations used have not been specified properly.

For example, in equation 3.20, as $\dot{X}$ is hypothesized to act upon Y_g through its effect on P_g and therefore on I/Y, the inclusion of $\dot{X}$, P_g and I/Y as determinants in equation 3.20 makes little sense. Kenen and Voivodas have implicitly adopted a Harrod-Domar framework by including I/Y as a determinant of Y_g in equation 3.20. It would have made more sense to begin by having Y_g = (1/k)(I/Y), where k is the incremental capital-output ratio, and then make I/Y a negative function of P_g, and P_g a positive function of $\dot{X}$, so that the estimating equation, in a general form, becomes:

$$Y_g = f(\dot{X}, AR, A) \tag{3.23}$$

Then there are the studies which have been carried out with even less care. An example is Lancieri (1978) who used Spearman rank correlation analysis to test for relationships between export instability, on the one hand, and the size of exports, the economic size of the developing countries, the per capita income, the growth rate of exports, the growth rate of GDP and the growth rate of investment, on the other hand, for a sample of developing countries for 1961-72. Only the relationships between export instability and the last three of the other variables are directly relevant to the debate on the effect of instability on economic growth. The simplistic statistical way in which the analysis has been carried out, without any attempt to spell out the theoretical relationships, would cast very serious doubt on the claim that the presence of a statistically significant Spearman rank correlation coefficient between instability and the growth rate of GDP shows that instability has been detrimental to growth.

A much more serious study was carried out by Voivodas (1974). This was an attempt to examine the effects of export instability on the imports of capital goods and it set out with an explicit framework, using the one provided by the Harrod-Domar growth model:

$$Y_g = (I/k)\ (I/Y) \tag{3.24}$$

where k is the incremental capital-output ratio. I/Y was then made to vary positively with d MK/Y, the change in the capital goods imports to income ratio, and inversely with the variance of the ratio itself, which was used as a proxy for export instability. In general form, the function is:

$$I/Y = f(d\ \overset{+}{MK}/Y, \text{var}\ \overset{-}{MK}/Y) \tag{3.25}$$

MK/Y itself was assumed to be a positive function of the change in the exports to GDP ratio (d X/Y) and of the change in the foreign capital inflow to GDP ratio (d F/Y):

$$MK/Y = f(d\ \overset{+}{X}/Y, d\ \overset{+}{F}/Y) \tag{3.26}$$

The estimating equation used, after a series of substitutions, was:

$$Y_g = f\,(\mathrm{d}\,\overset{+}{X}/Y,\ \mathrm{d}\,\overset{+}{F}/Y,\ \mathrm{var}\ \overset{-}{X}/Y,\ \mathrm{var}\ \overset{-}{F}/Y,\ \mathrm{cov}\ [X, \overset{-}{F}]/Y) \qquad (3.27)$$

This estimating equation has therefore been derived systematically, with each step of the process shown. Unfortunately the derivation is not quite consistent with the hypothesis examined. The hypothesis sees export instability as being responsible for an unpredictable supply of MK, which then creates bottlenecks at crucial points in the implementation of the investment programmes of those countries which depend heavily on the imports of capital goods. It would be more appropriate to write equation 3.25 as:

$$I/Y = f\,(\mathrm{d}\,M\overset{+}{K}/Y) \qquad (3.25a)$$

and equation (3.26) as:

$$MK/Y = f\,(\mathrm{d}\,\overset{+}{X}/Y,\ \mathrm{var}\ \overset{-}{X}/Y,\ \mathrm{var\ d}\ \overset{+}{F}/Y,\ \mathrm{var}\ \overset{-}{F}/Y) \qquad (3.26a)$$

The substitution of equations 3.25a and 3.26a into equation 3.24 will produce the following general form of the estimating equation:

$$Y_g = f\,(\mathrm{d}\,\overset{+}{X}/Y,\ \mathrm{var}\ \overset{-}{X}/Y,\ \mathrm{d}\,\overset{+}{F}/Y,\ \mathrm{and}\ \overset{-}{F}/Y) \qquad (3.27a)$$

This equation is different from equation 3.27, in not having a covariance term as an independent variable. This difference is important as it rids the estimating equation of a variable which has no distinct economic meaning *vis à vis* the instability issue, but which may capture some of the effects which are meant to be recorded by the two instability terms. What is important are the separate influences of export instability and foreign capital inflow instability (as measured by their respective variances), and not their joint instability (when account must be taken of their covariance as well).

That this is an important distinction is shown by the results obtained for equations 3.27 and 3.27a for a sample of twenty-nine developing countries over two periods, 1956-68 and 1956-73 (Lim, 1976). Export instability was shown to have no influence on economic growth when the covariance term was used, as in equation 3.27, but a significant adverse impact when the covariance term was excluded, as in equation 3.27a. Clearly, the covariance term captured some of the effects of instability, which were intended to be recorded by the export instability variable.

The point of this discussion is that the results obtained with the use of estimating equations that do not correspond much to either the spirit or the logic of the *a priori* arguments concerning export instability have to be treated with great caution. In extreme cases the results may have to be ignored. The policy-maker of a developing country with unstable export proceeds would do well to examine critically some of the procedures adopted by the existing studies and to return to the fundamentals of the *a priori* case before he makes up his mind or conducts his own study.

Use of different measures of instability

While it is accepted that instability refers to the short-term variations from the "normal" value and not simply as a coefficient of variation, there are different ways of measuring the "normal" value. Such differences could have been responsible for the different results obtained on the effects of export instability on growth.

Most often, the "normal" value is obtained as a trend value. In some cross-sectional studies, the shape of the trend line used, whether linear (Glezakos, 1973; Voivodas, 1974) or exponential (Lancieri, 1978), is imposed on all the countries in the sample, regardless of what each country's trend values may look like. In other cross-sectional studies, the best-fitting trend line for each country is used (Tan, 1983). The instability index, usually derived as the average of the annual normalized deviations of the actual values from the trend values, obtained with the use of the first undifferentiated approach, will not be accurate for a developing country whose actual trend line does not fit well with the imposed one. Under these conditions, the results obtained on the relationship between export instability and economic growth must have dubious value.

A good example of how a faulty measure of the instability index can produce misleading results can be found in the comment by Tan (1983) on a paper by Lam (1980). The index used by Lam for measuring export instability is the standard error of estimate normalized by the mean, with the standard error of estimate being obtained by taking the deviations of the values of exports from their trend values. The trend values were obtained by a linear regression of export values against time. Tan pointed out that the export values of the countries in the sample used are in fact not linearly related to time, and the imposition of a linear trend to non-linear data will produce two undesirable effects. First, it will give biased regression coefficients because of the presence of first-order auto-correlation in the residuals. Second, it will result in countries with higher export growth rates having larger standard errors of estimate.

It is this second effect that is important to the debate, for the instability index used by Lam contains a positive bias as countries with higher growth rates of exports will have higher export instability. Under these circumstances, the positive rank correlation coefficients obtained by Lam between export instability and export expansion are to be expected and cannot be interpreted as export instability having benefited export or economic growth. Tan re-estimated the instability indices for export earnings for the countries in Lam's sample by using a curvilinear trend line and found, after this correction for bias, that there was no statistically significant correlation between export instability and export expansion or domestic income expansion.

Export instability has also been measured using an instability index that is based on deviations from a moving average (World Bank, 1976). The use of such an index will also produce a positive bias between export instability and export growth because the higher the growth rate of exports is the higher will be the measured degree of export fluctuations. If export growth is positively related to growth of the GDP, then the spurious positive relationship between export instability and export growth will lead to an equally spurious positive link between export instability and economic growth.

Different studies have thus used quite different instability indices. Some of these indices produce biases which render the results obtained between export instability and economic growth somewhat dubious. It is quite possible that the difference in measuring instability is an important cause of the differences in results obtained.

Other weaknesses

Differences in the time-periods studied can also be a reason for the differences in results. The level of instability varies between periods of time (e.g. the 1970s was a much more unstable decade than the 1960s). If there is a threshold of instability beyond which the effects of instability can be particularly noticeable, then a study which concentrates on a more unstable period may show instability to be, say, harmful to growth while a study which looks at a more stable period may not capture any effect. When the results of one study contradict those of another, it is not always done on the basis of the same sample of developing countries over the same period of time.

The reasons given so far for the often contradictory results apply to all the three types of approaches. Problems associated with each of the three approaches have added to the general confusion created. The cross-country approach is by far the most popular, not because it has more intrinsic value than the other two, but because the data required are easily obtained from international sources. However, the ease with which data can be obtained should not hide a major weakness of the approach, which is its unwarranted assumption that the model used fits reasonably well all of the countries included in the sample. Even if the sample of developing countries has been carefully selected according to the requirements of the hypothesis to be tested, a heroic assumption has still to be made in the claim that what applies to all will apply equally to each individual country. The essence of the cross-country approach is that the countries are clustered together with little consideration for differences in their domestic economic structures. It is a convenient approach but one whose results have to be interpreted with great care.

These considerations would argue for an approach which examines each country individually. This can use the single-estimating-equation model popular with most of the cross-sectional studies or the nation-wide econometric and simulation model popular with recent studies. This country approach will enable the peculiarities of each developing country to be investigated. However, there are two major problems with this approach. The first is the severe data requirement, for unless long time-series are available, the analysis will reveal little about the relationship between instability and growth. This is particularly the case with the modelling study, for long time-series are needed for a large number of variables. The second problem concerns the shortage of statistical and modelling skills in developing countries generally to carry out econometric and simulation modelling. In many cases it is precisely these problems which have either encouraged or forced researchers to use the cross-sectional approach. The varying duration of the time-series and the differences in the level of sophistication of the analyses attempted might have been partly responsible for the contradictory results obtained.

New Empirical Analysis

The analysis so far suggests that the unavailability of reliable and relevant statistical data and the inadequacy of the technical approaches available have often combined to produce contradictory results on the effects of export instability on economic growth. The consequence of this combination of obstacles can be seen quite clearly in the following attempt to test for one of the alleged adverse effects of export instability on economic growth (Lim, 1987c).

This is the argument that export instability produces instability in government revenue which leads to instability in government expenditure. This instability in government expenditure is then seen to affect economic growth adversely in two ways. First, it makes the orderly implementation of development plans difficult. In order to avoid supply bottlenecks, scarce skilled personnel may have to be diverted from more important developmental tasks and the opportunity cost of this may be high. This argument therefore concentrates on the administrative problems and costs created by expenditure instability as a result of export instability.

The second reason for believing that expenditure instability is detrimental to economic growth is the adverse effect that expenditure instability has on investment. Public and private investment programmes complement each other to a large extent. For example, the availability of industrial estates at subsidized rates can influence industrial investment. Instability in public expenditure reduces the confidence that private investors have in the ability of the government to provide the necessary complementary public facilities. This results in the precautionary discounting of potential investment returns and so in a lowering of the investment level (Idachaba, 1975).

Export instability and economic growth

The aim is to test the effect of export instability on economic growth via its influence on investment, not to examine the administrative costs of export instability.

To ensure that a theoretically correct way of testing the hypothesis is adopted, we begin the formal explicit modelling by using the Harrod-Domar growth equation:

$$Y_g = (1/k)\,(I/Y) \qquad (3.24)$$

where Y_g is the growth rate of the real GDP, k the incremental capital-output ratio, and I/Y the domestic investment expenditure to GDP ratio.

I/Y is then made to vary inversely with instability in government expenditure ($\dot{E}$) because of precautionary discounting by private foreign and local investors:

$$I/Y = a - b\dot{E} \qquad (3.28)$$

Governments depend largely on their revenues for funding their expenditure programmes, so that instability in government revenue ($\dot{R}$) will be reflected by instability in government expenditure. The availability of foreign funds for the government weakens the relationship between revenue instability and expenditure instability as it provides the government with another source of funds for financing its expenditure programme. Thus the higher the government's foreign capital inflow as a proportion of GDP (F), the lower will be expenditure instability for a given revenue instability. Thus we have:

$$\dot{E} = c + d\,\dot{R} - e\,F \qquad (3.29)$$

$\dot{R}$ is hypothesized to vary positively with instability in export earnings ($\dot{X}$). Most of the economies of developing countries are dominated by the agricultural sector. The price elasticity of demand for, and the price elasticity of supply of, agricultural products are low. At the same time supply is unstable because of the vagaries of the weather and other natural factors. Demand is sensitive to changes in the income level, especially if the products are for export, so that shifts in demand occur frequently. These supply and demand conditions combine to produce severe price and income instability. This then produces government revenue instability because of the importance of the agricultural sector in the tax structure of developing countries and because of the widespread use of *ad valorem* export taxes for administrative efficiency and ease. Thus we have:

$$\dot{R} = f + g\,\dot{X} \qquad (3.30)$$

Through a series of substitutions, we obtain the following estimating equation:

$$Y_g = a_o - b_o\,\dot{X} + c_o\,F \qquad (3.31)$$

where $a_o = (a - bc - dbf)/k$, $b_o = bdg/k$, and $c_o = be/k$.

In the empirical analysis that follows we shall estimate not only equation 3.31 but also equations 3.28, 3.29 and 3.30 in order to test for the presence of the structural relationships underlying the postulated link between export instability and economic growth.

The testing for the underlying structural relationships is required to ensure that we are testing the hypothesis of precautionary discounting and not some other hypothesis arising out of the general argument against export instability. For example, it has been claimed that export instability produces inflation which then affects investment and therefore, growth adversely (Myrdal, 1956:238-52). Thus we have:

$$I/Y = h - iP + jF \tag{3.32}$$

$$P = l + m\dot{X} \tag{3.33}$$

where P is the rate of inflation and the other variables are as defined previously. I/Y is also made to depend on F because foreign capital inflows provide another source of funds for investment. The substitution of equation 3.33 into equation 3.32 and the substitution of the resulting equation into the Harrod-Domar growth equation 3.24 produces the following estimating equation:

$$Y_g = a_1 - b_1 \dot{X} + c_1 F \tag{3.34}$$

where $a_1 = (h - il)/k$, $b_1 = im/k$, and $c_1 = j/k$.

It can be seen that equation 3.34 is identical to equation 3.31 for estimating purposes. Yet the derivations of equations 3.34 and 3.31 show that two different aspects of the general argument against export instability are being tested. It makes nonsense of the theoretical distinction between the two hypotheses if the same estimating equation is used. In order to ensure that we are testing for the precautionary discounting of investment returns, the specific intermediate linkages between export instability and economic growth, as given by equations 3.28, 3.29 and 3.30, have to be estimated.

Empirical verification procedure

If the derivation of the estimating and structural equations has been carried out systematically and in a way that is consistent with the hypothesis, then the next step is to ensure that the empirical estimation of them is also carried out in the same correct manner.

From the comments made about the weaknesses of some of the existing empirical studies, it would appear that the hypothesis is best tested for a specific country over a long period. A cross-country approach is not desirable as it would have to assume, rather rashly, uniformity across countries in the effects of instability on growth, regardless of the differences between countries. A long period of analysis is required because these effects of instability are long-term ones which can only be captured by the statistical analysis if enough time is allowed for the effects to work their way through the economic system.

Unfortunately the time-series data required are not easily available for most developing countries. This is why most of the empirical studies have been cross-sectional ones. For the small number of case studies that have been carried out, the time period used is usually far too short for the results to be meaningful and to be of use to policy-makers. In the few studies where this is not the case, the results cannot be transferred equally to other countries, if the logic for using the case study approach is accepted. What then should the policy-makers of an economically unstable country with poor statistical data do under the circumstances?

It is possible that they can refer to the results for a country which has the same characteristics as their own. But the chances of finding such a study are very small, and the usefulness of the results would decrease the bigger the differences between the economic and non-economic circumstances of the two countries. If these differences are significant, then it might be better to rely on the results of a properly constructed and implemented cross-country study. These results would show the average of the different countries' responses to export instability and can provide a useful guide for policy formulation so long as the policy-makers are able to allow for their country's different circumstances.

It is in this spirit that equations 3.28, 3.29, 3.30 and 3.31 were estimated by ordinary least-squares regression analysis for a sample of forty-four developing countries for the period 1967-81. The first part of the period was one of relative international economic stability, the second one of relative instability following the massive increases in the price of oil in 1973 and 1978-79.

As the problems identified in the model represented by equations 3.24 and 3.28 to 3.31 are theoretically only of concern to those developing countries which have a large export sector and which are highly dependent on a few primary commodities for this export, the equations were also estimated for two sub-groups of countries (see Appendix 3.1). Sub-group I consists of those fourteen countries which have above-average export to GDP ratios and commodity concentration ratios. Sub-group II consists of those fifteen with below-average values for these two ratios. The expectation is that economic growth in the countries in sub-group I would be affected more by export instability than those in sub-group II.

The instability index used is the standard error of estimate normalized by the mean. The standard error of estimate is obtained by taking deviations of the value of the variable concerned (e.g. export earnings) from its trend values over a given period. The trend values are obtained by a simple linear or non-linear regression, whichever gives the better fit, of the export earnings against time. It is important that only the trend values from the best-fitting regression line are used. If a linear trend is imposed on the export values of a country that are not linearly related to time, it will produce biased regression coefficients because of the presence of first-order auto-correlation in the residuals. Also, it will result in countries with higher export growth rates having larger standard errors of estimate, and therefore higher export instability indices. If export growth is important for economic growth, the positive bias created will produce a spurious positive relationship between export instability and economic growth (Tan, 1983; Glezakos, 1973). $\dot{E}$, $\dot{R}$ and $\dot{X}$ are the instability indices for government expenditure, government revenue and export earnings respectively.

Both the linear and the logarithmic formulations of the functional relationships postulated by equations 3.28, 3.29, 3.30 and 3.31 were estimated. The linear formulation produces, in general, the better results. The results for the total sample of countries, obtained when the instability index was derived from the best-fitting trend lines, are given in Table 3.5. Table 3.6 presents the results for the countries in sub-group I and Table 3.7 the results for the countries in sub-group II. These tables also contain the results obtained when the instability index was derived from the second-best-fitting trend line. The regression coefficient for the export instability variable ($\dot{X}$) obtained with the use of the second-best-fitting trend line is expected to be positive and to be more significant than that obtained when $\dot{X}$ was estimated using the best-fitting trend line because of the positive bias created.

Empirical results

Table 3.5 shows that, for the total sample of forty-four developing countries, export instability produced revenue instability (equation 3.30) which, in turn, brought about expenditure instability (equation 3.29), in spite of the cushioning effect of foreign capital inflow. However, there is no evidence that all these things led in turn to the precautionary discounting of investment returns (equation 3.28). The coefficients obtained for $\dot{E}$ in equation 3.28 are not statistically significant, even though they have the expected negative sign.

The results for equation 3.31 show that export instability was detrimental to economic growth, when the second-best-fitting trend

Table 3.5: Cross-country linear regressions explaining I/Y, $\dot{E}$, $\dot{R}$ and Y_g: total sample (44 countries), 1967-81

Dependent variable	I/Y Equ. 3.28		$\dot{E}$ Equ. 3.29		$\dot{R}$ Equ. 3.30		Y_g Equ. 3.31	
Independent variable	Best-fit trend line	2nd-best-fit trend line	Best-fit trend line	2nd-best-fit trend line	Best-fit trend line	2nd-best-fit trend line	Best-fit trend line	2nd-best-fit trend line
Constant	20.708	21.364	0.056	0.111	0.016	0.014	5.040	3.326
	(19.884)*	(16.825)*	(1.359)	(2.717)*	(0.229)	(0.150)	(6.021)*	(4.021)*
$\dot{E}$	-2.744	-3.406						
	(-0.907)	(-1.274)						
$\dot{R}$			1.040	0.970				
			(7.984)*	(10.713)*				
F			-0.551	-0.003			-0.040	-0.011
			(-0.107)	(-0.752)			(-0.673)	(-0.194)
$\dot{X}$					1.102	1.221	1.760	7.682
					(2.407)*	(3.312)*	(0.406)	(2.645)*
R^2	0.019	0.037	0.619	0.746	0.148	0.207	0.018	0.158
F- ratio	0.823	1.623	33.321	60.195	7.325	10.972	0.377	3.842

Notes: Figures in parentheses are the t values of the regression coefficients. Statistical significance at the 1 and 5 per cent confidence levels are indicated by * and ** respectively. The same applies to Tables 3.6 and 3.7.

Data for the analysis here and in Tables 3.6 and 3.7 are taken from the first, second and third editions of The World Bank, *World Tables* (Baltimore, Johns Hopkins University Press).

Table 3.6: Cross-country linear regressions explaining I/Y, $\dot{E}$, $\dot{R}$ and Y_g: sub-group I (14 countries), 1967-81

Dependent variable	I/Y Equ. 3.28		$\dot{E}$ Equ. 3.29		$\dot{R}$ Equ. 3.30		Y_g Equ. 3.31	
Independent variable	Best-fit trend line	2nd-best-fit trend line	Best-fit trend line	2nd-best-fit trend line	Best-fit trend line	2nd-best-fit trend line	Best-fit trend line	2nd-best-fit trend line
Constant	19.440	23.594	0.198	0.333	-0.004	0.039	4.752	2.385
	(7.059)*	(5.147)*	(2.409)*	(4.501)*	(-0.098)	(0.537)	(2.863)*	(1.279)
$\dot{E}$	2.999	-10.635						
	(0.259)	(-0.793)						
$\dot{R}$			0.290	0.167				
			(0.718)	(0.680)				
F			-0.006	-0.008			0.028	0.079
			(-0.963)	(-1.823)**			(0.305)	(0.869)
$\dot{X}$					1.102	0.982	-4.040	6.592
					(3.878)*	(3.048)*	(-0.484)	(0.918)
R^2	0.006	0.050	0.134	0.281	0.556	0.436	0.044	0.093
F- ratio	0.067	0.629	0.853	2.148	15.040	9.287	0.253	0.564

Table 3.7: Cross-country linear regressions explaining I/Y, $\dot{E}$, $\dot{R}$ and Y_g: sub-group II (15 countries), 1967-81

Dependent variable	I/Y Equ. 3.28		$\dot{E}$ Equ. 3.29		$\dot{R}$ Equ. 3.30		Y_g Equ. 3.31	
Independent variable	Best-fit trend line	2nd-best-fit trend line	Best-fit trend line	2nd-best-fit trend line	Best-fit trend line	2nd-best-fit trend line	Best-fit trend line	2nd-best-fit trend line
Constant	22.475	22.627	-0.022	0.001	-0.005	0.010	5.482	4.567
	(14.169)*	(11.654)*	(-0.714)*	(0.025)	(-0.426)	(0.055)*	(5.365)*	(4.423)*
$\dot{E}$	-4.463	-3.127						
	(-1.012)	(-0.817)						
$\dot{R}$			1.140	1.084				
			(17.799)*	(16.482)*				
F			0.013	0.010			-0.034	0.007
			(1.775)**	(1.065)			(-0.197)	(0.041)
$\dot{X}$					1.679	1.400	1.849	4.600
					(2.245)*	(2.077)*	(0.397)	(1.412)
R^2	0.073	0.049	0.964	0.958	0.279	0.249	0.020	0.149
F- ratio	1.025	0.667	159.123	136.488	5.042	4.313	0.125	1.049

line was used to derive $\dot{X}$. When the best-fitting trend line was used, export instability had no effect on economic growth. This shows quite clearly that a spurious positive relationship between export instability and economic growth will be obtained whenever an incorrect method of estimating instability is used.

Table 3.6 shows that, for those countries with above-average dependence on exports and on a few primary commodities (sub-group I countries), export instability produced revenue instability. However, this was not translated into expenditure instability nor into a slowing down of the rate of economic growth. The presence of government foreign capital inflow had weakened the link between revenue instability, induced by export instability, and expenditure instability. As investment is expected to be adversely affected by expenditure instability, the absence of expenditure instability did not produce a lowering of investment and, hence, of economic growth.

For those countries with below-average exports to GDP ratios and commodity concentration ratios (sub-group II countries), export instability did lead to revenue instability (Table 3.7). This produced, in turn, expenditure instability but not lower economic growth.

The results for the two sub-groups of countries are, therefore, not all that different. However, it would not be possible to argue from this that countries with quite different production and export structures are not affected differently by export instability. The sample sizes (fourteen and fifteen) are too small for meaningful results to be obtained.

Concluding remarks

After taking due care with the derivation of the estimating equations and with the actual estimation of them, we see that there is no evidence that export instability encouraged the precautionary discounting of investment returns for a group of forty-four developing countries over the period 1967-81. Export instability did produce revenue instability which, in turn, brought about expenditure instability. But the chain reaction went no further than this.

However, we cannot say from this analysis that export instability is not a development issue for those developing countries that are economically unstable and that have a narrow economic base. The sample used includes developing countries which do not possess such characteristics because to have excluded them would give a sample size that is far too small for meaningful statistical results to be obtained.

Herein lies one of the problems of empirical work in the social sciences. Even if the derivation of the model had been properly done, the correct empirical testing of it requires data that is simply not available. The only certain result that has been obtained from our analysis is that the positive and significant relationship between export instability and economic growth was due to the use of an inappropriate method of measuring export instability. This is an important finding as it suggests that studies which show export instability to be beneficial to economic growth might have done so because of a technical error.

It is clear from our own analysis and from that of other studies that the results do not overwhelmingly support the case for or against export instability. However, the effort has not been wasted as it has pointed out the problems with the statistical testing of the relationship between export instability and economic growth and the directions that such testing must take for the results to be more acceptable.

Thus it has shown that the case cannot be settled by doing a head count of the number of studies supporting one school of thought or another, though if this approach was taken, there would be more studies showing instability to be harmful to growth. A more sensible approach in extracting some conclusions from the empirical studies would be to judge the results of the studies by the care with which they have chosen their countries or samples of countries, and tested their hypotheses. The results of those studies which have been cavalier in any of these two areas may have to be discounted.

If these two criteria were used in assessing the existing cross-country studies, it may be concluded that those studies which are more careful in their choice of countries and which adopt a more theoretically correct way of testing the hypotheses have shown export instability to be detrimental to economic growth. There are, of course, cross-country studies which may not be criticized on these two grounds and which show instability to be beneficial to growth (e.g. Knudsen and Yotopoulos, 1976; Lim, 1980). To the extent that these show export instability to have produced higher savings and investment rates, there need not be any inconsistency with our conclusion. It is not too difficult to imagine cases, under uncertainty, where higher savings end up as investment in areas which are not conducive to the long-term growth of a country and which will ultimately reduce its rate of economic growth.

Views of Governments and International Organizations

In sharp contrast to the academic literature, an examination of the development plans of primary-producing developing countries will show that most of these have, implicitly or explicity, accepted the validity of some or all of the *a priori* arguments against export instability. However, some of them have appeared to be concerned about instability only because they have mistakenly assumed it to be the same as the issue of a secular decline in export prices and earnings.

Most of the important international organizations dealing with economic development have also assumed that export instability is bad for economic growth, as they have been operating for some time schemes to either reduce the extent of export instability or lessen the impact of such instability on growth. The most important of these is the compensatory financing facility of the International Monetary Fund (IMF-CFF). This was established in 1963 to compensate largely primary-producing developing countries for temporary shortfalls in export earnings, when such countries run into balance-of-payments difficulties of a short-term character. The compensation is to reduce the short-run fluctuations in export earnings and so hopefully to mitigate the adverse impact of export instability on the planning process. The average annual drawing from the scheme during 1976-83 was, in Special Drawing Rights (SDRs), the unit of account issued to governments by the International Monetary Fund, 1.42 billion.

The European Community operates a commodity-specific compensatory financing scheme for sixty-six developing countries in Africa, the Caribbean and the Pacific (the ACP countries). This is the scheme known as Stabex and covers primarily agricultural products. Under the third ACP-EEC Lomé Convention, US$821 million have been set aside for Stabex to reduce the harmful effects of the instability in export earnings.

The World Bank has been more concerned with the slow growth, rather than the instability, of export earnings. However, it too has recognized the problems that could arise from instability ever since the early 1960s. In 1979 it produced a joint report with the IMF which proposed that temporary shortfalls in export earnings should be dealt with by an improved IMF-CFF, while medium-term shortfalls should be tackled by the World Bank through the granting of structural adjustment loans (IMF-World Bank, 1979).

International commodity agreements have been set up for such products as cocoa, coffee, rubber and tin. The stabilization of prices has been the major concern of these agreements, in implicit recognition of the detrimental effects of the revenue instability that is presumed to result from price instability. The same reason underlies the attempt to set up the Common Fund of the Integrated Programme for Commodities in UNCTAD. If the scheme comes into operation, it will attempt to stabilize the prices of a number of primary commodities by providing the funds to run buffer stocks.

In 1985 an Expert Group set up by UNCTAD on compensatory financing of export earning shortfalls (UNCTAD, 1985) accepted the argument that export instability was bad for economic growth. It found that supply fluctuations were more important than price fluctuations in bringing about instability in export earnings. It then pointed out that the first-best solution is to deal with the causes, in this case supply-oriented, and not the effects of export instability. As the present international programmes do not deal adequately, if at all, with the causes of commodity supply instability, the report recommended the establishment of a new compensatory facility which operates in a different manner to that of the IMF-CFF.

The relevant international organizations have therefore accepted that export instability is detrimental to economic growth. These range from the more conservative IMF and the World Bank, to the middle-of-the-road EEC and the more radical UNCTAD. They only differ in the way they approach the issue. By providing short-term balance-of-payments assistance to maintain the import capacity of countries affected by an export shortfall, the IMF addresses one of the effects of export instability and not the causes of it at the sectoral level. In contrast, the Expert Group of UNCTAD argues for the reverse approach. The World Bank also sees the solution to export instability as dealing with the root causes of instability at the sectoral level. However, by tackling the issue through structural adjustment programmes, it sees the instability problem as only one of a number of related problems encountered by developing countries.

The approach taken by the various international commodity agreements and by the proposed Common Fund of UNCTAD is to stabilize prices in the hope of stabilizing earnings and hence, of mitigating the adverse effects of instability. Stabex is a commodity-specific compensatory financing scheme but its transfers are, in reality, used as foreign aid.

The next part of the study examines the *modus operandi* of the two existing compensatory programmes to deal with the issue of export instability and economic growth - the compensatory financing facility of the IMF and the Stabex programme of the European Community. The ability of these schemes to (i) produce stable export earnings, on which the prospects for faster economic growth are seen to critically depend, (ii) tackle the causes of export instability, and (iii) deal with the economic problems created by instability will be assessed.

Appendix 3.1: Countries by Export/GDP and Commodity Concentration Ratios, 1967-81

The forty-four countries can be divided into four sub-groups:

Sub-group I - those whose export/GDP (X/Y) ratios and commodity concentration (CC) ratios are above average: these numbered fourteen.

Sub-group II - those whose X/Y and CC ratios are less than average: these numbered fifteen.

Sub-group III - those with above-average values for the X/Y ratio and below-average values for the CC ratio: these numbered five.

Sub-group IV - those with below-average values for the X/Y ratio and above-average values for the CC ratio: these numbered ten.

The countries under these four sub-groups are shown on the following pages. The commodity concentration ratio is the current value of the three major primary commodities in the exports of a country as a percentage of the total current value of its merchandise exports.

Country	Export/GDP ratio (%) 1967-81 Average	Commodity concentration ratio (%) 1967-81 Average
Total	28.1	55.2
Sub-group I	42.1	71.1
Costa Rica	31.1	64.3
El Salvador	29.1	65.0
Fiji	47.0	62.7
Gambia	42.5	78.6
Guyana	55.9	74.5
Honduras	29.7	65.9
Kuwait	67.7	68.9
Liberia	54.6	92.1
Malaysia	46.4	60.3
Mauritania	46.9	86.6
Mauritius	44.2	83.3
Nicaragua	28.7	60.0
Panama	37.4	57.8
Sri Lanka	28.1	75.4

(continued over)

Appendix 3.1 (continued)

Country	Export/GDP ratio (%) 1967–81 Average	Commodity concentration ratio (%) 1967–81 Average
Sub-group II	16.9	38.8
Greece	13.0	31.6
Guatemala	18.2	52.0
India	4.9	19.9
Mexico	9.5	34.9
Morocco	20.1	40.0
Pakistan	11.1	29.1
Papua New Guinea	26.5	44.2
Paraguay	12.9	49.5
Peru	16.3	51.5
Philippines	19.4	47.4
Portugal	25.6	3.7
Tanzania	21.2	46.1
Thailand	20.2	43.0
Tunisia	26.9	51.3
Turkey	7.8	37.6
Sub-group III	44.4	41.3
Barbados	60.9	39.3
Cameroon	28.8	52.3
Cyprus	40.9	27.2
Iran	28.4	49.4
Swaziland	62.9	38.5
Sub-group IV	17.2	69.4
Bolivia	19.9	65.2
Colombia	13.3	70.4
Ecuador	18.7	74.9
Indonesia	16.0	64.7
Mali	18.1	81.1
Nigeria	21.5	75.3
Sudan	15.4	63.0
Togo	24.3	76.5
Upper Volta	9.9	67.0
Uruguay	14.9	56.0

Part II
Compensatory Financing Schemes

4
IMF-CFF: Description of its Operations

Aim of IMF-CFF

The compensatory financing facility (CFF) was established by the International Monetary Fund (IMF) in 1963 to provide "additional assistance to member countries experiencing balance-of-payments difficulties arising from export shortfalls, provided the latter are temporary and largely attributable to circumstances beyond the member's control. Ideally the facility should enable a member to borrow when its export earnings and financial reserves are low and to repay when they are high, so that its import capacity is unaffected by fluctuations in export earnings caused by external events" (Goreux, 1980: 3).

Without such a compensatory financing system, a member country with an export shortfall, low reserves and no access to international capital markets would be forced to restrict its imports and/or increase its balance-of-payments deficit. Such actions would "not only adversely affect the economic development of the country concerned but would also aggravate any balance-of-payments difficulties being experienced by its trading partners" (Goreux, 1980: 9). The establishment of the IMF-CFF would obviate the need for such actions on the part of the country concerned and would therefore help both it and its trading partners maintain their rates of economic growth.

The facility is open to all members of the IMF but the main users are members which are developing countries. The scheme therefore aims to maintain the import capacity of those developing countries with balance-of-payments difficulties activated by temporary export shortfalls, which are themselves caused by external factors.

The IMF-CFF was replaced by the IMF's compensatory and contingency financing facility (IMF-CCFF) in August 1988. This and the following chapter will assess the operation of the IMF-CFF.

Rules of Operation

The concept behind the IMF-CFF is simple. The facility will lend to countries in years when their export earnings are below what can be expected from the trend. These countries should repay the facility when their export earnings rise above the trend. If the differences between the actual and the trend values are accurately measured, then the export earnings net of IMF-CFF transactions of a participating country will be more stable than its unadjusted export earnings. Its import capacity will therefore fluctuate less and its economic growth less adversely affected.

To make the scheme operational, rules were drawn up concerning compensatory drawings and their repayment. For the former, the most important rules deal with the coverage of the scheme, the calculation of the trend and the shortfall, access, and the qualifying criteria. For the latter, the most important are concerned with the terms and the period of repayment and the interest charged on the outstanding drawings.

Coverage

When the scheme began in 1963, export proceeds referred to merchandise exports. In 1979 the coverage was expanded to include workers' remittances and income from tourism, in recognition of the important role that these two played in the earning of foreign exchange. The world food crisis of 1972-74 led to massive increases in the cost of cereal imports for many developing countries and a subsequent cutback in their imports of other essential goods. This led eventually to the decision in May 1981 to include cereal imports in the scheme, so that countries can obtain assistance in financing temporary increases in the cost of importing cereals (Ezekiel, 1985).

A member country can choose to base its request for compensatory drawings on export proceeds that include or exclude workers' remittances and earnings from tourism. However, once a choice is made it is bounded by it for the next five years. In addition, a member country can base its request on data that include cereal imports. Its total compensatory drawing would then be equal to the net amount of the export shortfall and the cereal import excess. Once the decision is taken, it is binding for three years.

Trend calculation

The amount that a member country can draw from the facility is limited by the amount of the estimated export shortfall, subject to a quota limit and the requirements of need and of co-operation with the IMF. The estimated shortfall is the amount by which export earnings in the shortfall year are below their medium-term value, defined as the five-year geometric average of export earnings centred on the shortfall year. As the shortfall year is normally the latest twelve-month period for which actual export data are available, export earnings for the two post-shortfall years are projected by the IMF in conjunction with the participating country.

This technique for estimating the medium-term trend of export earnings has only been in use since 1979. In 1963 the trend was obtained by first giving weights of 0.25 to export earnings in each of the two pre-shortfall years and one of 0.50 to export earnings in the shortfall year, and then using forecasts for the two post-shortfall years. The arithmetic average of export earnings for the five years centred on the shortfall year was used as the estimate of the medium-term trend value. In 1966 the weighting system was dropped in favour of a largely qualitative method, with upper and lower limits being placed on the forecasts. In 1975 an extrapolation technique for estimating the trend was introduced but this was never used and was abandoned in 1979, when the existing system was introduced. The decision to change to a geometric average was taken after analysis showed that the nominal value of export earnings tends to increase geometrically (i.e. at a constant rate) rather than arithmetically (i.e. by a constant amount).

All the calculations have been carried out in nominal terms. Considerations have been given at various times to carry out the exercise in real terms but on each occasion the proposal has been rejected. The usual reason given is that reliable import price values are not available for all countries. For those countries that do have reliable import price indices there is usually a long delay in their publication. The suggestion of using a common price deflator for all countries has also been rejected. All countries do not have import patterns that reflect the weights used in the common deflator, so the calculation would not produce a more desirable level of drawing than an exercise conducted in nominal terms.

Access

The amount that can be drawn from the facility cannot be greater than the calculated net shortfall or 83 per cent of the member's quota in the IMF. The same quota limit applies to the drawing for cereal imports, but if considered jointly with export shortfall drawings the limit is raised to 105 per cent of the quota.

In 1963 the limit was only 25 per cent of the member's quota. This was raised to 50 per cent in 1966, with drawings in any twelve-month period limited to 25 per cent of the quota. A two-tranche system was also introduced then, where a stricter test was imposed on drawings that exceeded 25 per cent of the quota. The next development took place in 1969, with the establishment of the buffer stock financing facility (BSFF), and a joint limit of 75 per cent of the quota was imposed on drawings from the IMF-CFF and the BSFF.

In 1975 this joint ceiling was removed and the limit on the IMF-CFF itself was increased to 75 per cent of the quota, with no more than 50 per cent being possible in any twelve-month period. The threshold for the upper tranche co-operation scheme was also raised to 50 per cent, which is the position today.

In 1979 the limit on drawings on the IMF-CFF was raised to 100 per cent of the quota and the constraint on drawings in any twelve-month period was removed. In 1981 when the financing of excesses in cereal imports was introduced, the same 100 per cent quota limit was applied, with a joint limit of 125 per cent of the quota on export shortfall and cereal drawings.

The present limits of 83 per cent of the quota for each of the two drawings and of 105 per cent for the joint drawing do not represent a tightening of the scheme. In 1984 the quotas of IMF members were increased very substantially and the separate and joint limits were adjusted downward to produce more or less the same absolute level of drawings.

The scheme allows early drawings to be made. This enables members to use estimated data in the shortfall year for up to six months in the case of merchandise exports and for up to twelve months for workers' remittances, tourism earnings and cereal imports. In essence, this permits members which take an inordinately long time in producing trade statistics to use the facility earlier and at a time of need. The same arrangement allows for over-compensation, as a result of inaccurate estimates, to be dealt with by the member re-purchasing the amount promptly.

In nominal terms, the total potential supply of drawings from the IMF-CFF has increased very markedly since its establishment in 1963. For the 120 developing countries in the IMF, the potential supply, obtained by multiplying their aggregate quota by the quota limits on export shortfall drawings, increased ten-fold from SDR 2 billion in 1963 to SDR 20 billion in 1984. Over the same period the total export earnings of developing countries increased about twenty-fold.

Qualifying criteria

To qualify for compensatory financing, three criteria have to be satisfied. The first is that there must be a balance-of-payments need. The second is that the shortfall in export earnings or the excess in cereal imports must be temporary and largely beyond the control of the member country. The third is that the IMF must be satisfied that the member country will co-operate with it in finding appropriate solutions to the balance-of-payments problems.

For requests that would push the drawing above 50 per cent of the quota (the upper tranche), the IMF must be satisfied that the member has been co-operating with it in the past in finding appropriate programmes to tackle the balance-of-payments difficulties.

The guidelines on co-operation, whether in terms of the willingness to co-operate with the IMF (the lower tranche) or of having co-operated with it (the upper tranche), have remained basically unchanged since their introduction in 1966. However, in the implementation of them, it has not always been possible to maintain the distinction between the more lenient requirement of the lower tranche and the harder one at the upper tranche.

Repayment

In order to draw on the compensatory financing facility, a member must have simultaneously an export shortfall and a balance-of-payments need. However, symmetry is not pursued in the repayment operation, as there is no requirement to repurchase when the member has an export surplus and the ability to repay. A grace period covers the first two years after the drawing is made. The repayments are made in equal quarterly instalments after that and must be completed within five years of the drawing. This is the same arrangement as the repurchase under the normal credit tranches and, as with this, there is only an expectation that the repurchase of the drawings will be accelerated when the member's balance-of-payments and reserves position improves. Such an improvement is seen to have taken place if the member's position is judged to be strong enough for inclusion in the quarterly designation plans or the operational budget.

The reasons for not seeking symmetry is that it would have required forecasting the export earnings of all countries with outstanding drawings at regular intervals, which is difficult, and an agreement between creditor and debtor on the forecasts that would lead to a repurchase, which is even more difficult.

There are instances where the data on export earnings for the shortfall year are not complete and estimates have to be used. When the use of such data results in the underestimation of the export earnings in the shortfall year and therefore in over-compensation, the member has to repurchase the excess promptly. The interest on the outstanding drawings is now 6.6 per cent per year. In addition, there is a service charge of 0.5 per cent for every drawing made.

A Hypothetical Drawing

It will be useful to work through a hypothetical request for a drawing from the IMF-CFF. First, to see how the various rules are brought into play and, second, to provide the basis for assessing the ability of the facility to stabilize export earnings and ultimately to promote economic growth.

The example, taken from Goreux (1980), concerns country X which obtains most of its export earnings from three primary commodities: coffee, tea and sugar. These are commodities with low price elasticities of supply and demand and subject to frequent and large shifts in their supply and demand.

In February 1980 country X requested a purchase of SDR 10 million from the IMF-CFF because of a shortfall in export earnings in the twelve-month period which ended on 30 September 1979. The country had a quota in the IMF of SDR 20 million and already had an outstanding drawing from the facility of SDR 10 million. The request in February 1980 of SDR 10 million was therefore the maximum that country X could obtain.

The Executive Board of the IMF then asked for an IMF staff report to establish the amount that country X could draw and whether it could satisfy the qualifying criteria of having a balance-of-payments need, a shortfall that is temporary and outside the control of the country, and a willingness to co-operate with the IMF in finding appropriate policies for solving its balance-of-payments problems.

Table 4.1 shows the balance-of-payments position for country X over the period 1977-80. The data for 1977 and 1978 were actual, that for 1979 provisional, and that for 1980 projected. Country X had a balance-of-payments surplus of SDR 42 million in 1977, and gross official reserves which would enable it to buy twenty-four weeks' worth of imports. By normal standards, these figures show country X to have a healthy balance-of-payments and reserves position in 1977.

However, things took a sharp turn for the worse in 1978 and 1979, when balance-of-payments deficits of SDR 23 million and SDR 38 million respectively were registered. The 1979 deficit was partly financed by a drawing from the IMF-CFF of SDR 10 million and an accumulation of payment arrears of SDR 4 million, but the size of the deficit was so large that the government had to run down its gross official reserves by SDR 24 million. The result was that the reserves stood at only SDR 34 million, which was equivalent to only seven weeks' worth of imports.

Table 4.1: Country X: balance-of-payments 1977-80 (millions of SDR)

		Calendar Years			
		1977	1978	1979	1980
A	**Current Account**	-31.9	-100.2	-125.9	-112.0
	Trade balance	14.4	-61.2	-61.8	-69.0
	exports	171.1	149.3	166.0	193.0
	imports	-156.7	-210.5	-227.8	-262.0
	Services	-68.1	-74.9	-106.8	-95.0
	Unrequited transfers	21.8	35.9	42.7	52.0
B	**Capital Account**	74.0	77.0	87.8	100.0
C	**Overall Balance (A + B)**	42.1	-23.2	-38.1	-12.0
D	**Financing**	-42.1	23.2	38.1	12.0
	Accumulation of arrears	-	3.2	4.0	-
	Increase in IMF-CFF credit	-	-	10.0	10.0
	Reduction in net official reserves:				
	increase in liabilities	-	5.9	-	-
	reduction in assets	42.1	14.1	24.1	2.0
E	**Gross Official Reserves**	72.2	58.1	34.0	32.0
	In weekly equivalent of imports	24.1	14.4	7.4	6.6

Source: Goreux (1980), p. 58.

The projected figures show that exports would rise in 1980 to produce a lower balance-of-payments deficit of SDR 12 million. However, the gross official reserves were not expected to rise that year, even if the request for a drawing of SDR 10 million from the IMF-CFF was granted. This would reduce the reserves to a level which would buy only 6.6 weeks' worth of imports.

The IMF staff report decided that there was a balance-of-payments need and that the request for an IMF-CFF drawing was consistent with this need. It was also discovered that country X had been operating with the IMF to find appropriate policies for solving its balance-of-payments problems. Thus the stricter test of co-operation which would have to apply, as country X's request would push its drawing to more than 50 per cent of its quota, would be met.

The next step was to decide whether the shortfall in export earnings which ended on 30 September 1979 was a temporary one, and whether country X could request a purchase of SDR 10 million. This would require a detailed analysis of the country's export performance.

The actual and projected total export earnings for 1974-81, as well as the earnings from the three most important items, are given in Table 4.2. Total export earnings fell by 5.9 per cent in the shortfall year, but were projected to recover strongly in the two post-shortfall years (20.1 per cent and 14.3 per cent respectively). More than 40 per cent of the shortfall was caused by a fall in earnings from coffee. This shortfall in earnings from coffee, and indeed from sugar, was due entirely to a temporary fall in the price. The volume of coffee and sugar exported in the shortfall year was, in fact, higher than the trend value. As country X accounted for only a small share of the world's exports of coffee, sugar and tea, the shortfall resulting from temporary price falls was seen to be outside its control.

The table shows that, on the basis of projections made on earnings for the period October 1979 - September 1981, the shortfall amounted to SDR 18.4 million when the geometric average was used. However, as the previous shortfall year, ending in March 1979, and the current one, ending in September 1979, overlapped by six months, the minimum shortfall required for an SDR 10 million drawing is only SDR 15 million. This is less than the estimated shortfall of SDR 18.4 million and country X could therefore purchase up to SDR 10 million, which would raise its outstanding drawings to 100 per cent of its quota.

Actual Drawings from the IMF-CFF

The drawings, repurchases and outstanding drawings under the IMF-CFF for the period January 1963 to December 1988 are given in Table 4.3. Although the scheme was established in 1963 it was not until its conditions were liberalized in December 1975 that substantial assistance could be given. Thus over the first thirteen years of its operation, the total amount of drawings was only SDR 1.22 billion, (less than SDR 100 million per year, which was very small in relation to the total export earnings of its members).

Table 4.2: Country X: export earnings and shortfalls by major commodities, 1974-81

	1974	1975	1976	1977	1978	1979	1980	1981	Shortfalls Geometric	Shortfalls Arithmetic
(Million SDRs)										
Total Exports	72.4	95.2	107.0	150.9	154.8	145.7	175.0	200.0	18.4	19.6
Coffee	31.6	38.5	53.7	76.1	89.9	81.0	93.4	106.1	7.7	8.3
Tea	15.8	20.5	22.8	40.8	26.7	27.8	30.2	34.2	3.8	4.1
Sugar	2.6	12.8	11.5	16.0	12.9	14.6	21.9	25.6	3.0	3.6
Others	22.4	23.4	19.0	18.0	25.3	22.3	29.5	34.1	2.9	3.5
(Annual Rate of Percentage Change in Earnings from Previous Year)										
Total Exports		31.5	12.4	41.0	2.6	-5.9	20.1	14.3		
Coffee		21.8	39.5	41.7	48.8	-9.9	15.3	13.6		
Tea		29.7	11.2	78.9	-34.6	4.1	8.6	13.2		
Sugar		392.3	-10.2	39.1	-19.4	13.2	50.0	16.9		
Others		4.5	-18.8	5.6	-24.9	-11.9	32.3	15.6		

Source: Goreux (1980), p. 61.

Table 4.3: Drawings, repurchases and outstanding drawings under the IMF-CFF[1]
(January 1963-December 1988), (millions of SDRs)

	Drawings			Repurchases			Outstanding drawings (end of period)		
	All IMF members	Developed countries [2]	Developing countries	All IMF members	Developed countries [2]	Developing countries	All IMF members	Developed countries[2]	Developing countries
1963 Decision									
1963	76	-	76	-	-	-	76	-	76
1964	-	-	-	-	-	-	76	-	76
1965	11	-	11	-	-	-	87	-	87
1966 Decision									
1966	24	-	24	16	-	16	96	-	96
1967	198	33	165	18	-	18	261	33	228
1968	69	4	65	78	29	49	251	8	243
1969	13	-	13	37	-	37	227	8	219
1970	3	-	3	97	8	89	132	-	132
1971	70	-	70	70	-	70	132	-	132
1972	299	-	299	51	-	51	380	-	380
1973	113	-	113	34	-	34	460	-	460
1974	107	-	107	32	-	32	535	-	535
1975	239	51	188	51	-	51	722	51	671
1976 Decision									
1976	2308	787	1521	317	-	317	2713	837	1876
1977	241	29	212	187	-	187	2756	866	1890
1978	578	171	407	387	86	301	2921	952	1969

(continued over)

Table 4.3 (continued)

	Drawings			Repurchases			Outstanding drawings (end of period)		
	All IMF members	Developed countries [2]	Developing countries	All IMF members	Developed countries [2]	Developing countries	All IMF members	Developed countries [2]	Developing countries
1976 Decision (continued)									
1979 [3]	279	139	140	353	31	322	2847	1059	1788
1979 Decision									
1979 [4]	293	-	293	290	189	101	2850	870	1980
1980	980	139	841	1039	381	658	2791	627	2164
1981	1243	-	1243	762	229	533	3272	399	2873
1982	2628	658	1970	502	129	373	5398	927	4471
1983	2839	267	2572	708	148	560	7529	1046	6483
1984	216	55	161	865	104	761	7480	996	6484
1985	929	-	929	1336	17	1319	6987	979	6008
1986	568	-	568	2151	332	1819	5404	647	4757
1987	1168	-	1168	2211	468	1743	4375	179	4196
1988	730	-	730	1223	179	1044	3883	-	3883

Source: IMF (1984), p. 7 and IMF Research Department.

1 Includes drawings under the cereal facility.
2 Includes industrial countries as defined in the International Monetary Fund's International Financial Statistics (IFS), plus Botswana, Lesotho, South Africa, Swaziland, Greece, Malta, Portugal, Yugoslavia and Israel.
3 January-July 1979.
4 August-December 1979.

The five general quota increases, the three increases in the quota limits of CFF drawings, the expansion of commodity coverage, the abolition of annual limits and drawings, and the elimination of limits on projections over the years, especially since 1975, have transformed the operation of the facility. Thus the average drawings per year over the period 1976-88 came to SDR 1.2 billion, which was about the same as the entire amount drawn in the previous thirteen years.

It is clear from the table that the size and the timing of the drawings depend very largely on changes in the international economic system. Thus the drawing in 1976, SDR 2.31 billion, was very high, not only because of the 1975 liberalization of the facility but also because it came in the wake of the 1975 recession. The recession in 1981-82 was also followed by very heavy purchases in 1982 (SDR 2.63 billion) and 1983 (SDR 2.84 billion).

Even though the facility is open to all of the members of the IMF, the major users have been the developing countries. Table 4.4 shows that such countries accounted for 86 per cent of the aggregate drawings over the period 1976 - 88. They were also responsible for the major part, 84 per cent, of the total credit extended by the IMF.

Table 4.4 also shows that the drawings from the CFF accounted for 25 per cent of all the credit provided by the IMF. The other 75 per cent were channelled through the credit tranches and extended IMF facility, the oil facility, and the buffer stock financing facility. This three to one ratio in favour of non-CFF credit applies to both the developed and the developing countries.

Table 4.5 shows that the eighty-eight drawings over the period 1976-79, following the 1975 liberalization decision, totalled SDR 3.41 billion. This was about 50 per cent of the calculated shortfalls. There were 152 drawings over the period 1979 - December 1988. These amounted to SDR 8.43 billion, which came to 62 per cent of the estimated shortfall in export earnings. The percentage of drawings to shortfalls increased consistently over the 1981-83 period, from 49 per cent in 1981 to 63 per cent in 1982 and 75 per cent in 1983. This prompted the IMF to conclude that "according to this measure, therefore, the capacity of the CFF to mitigate the adverse effects of export fluctuations is shown to have increased during a period of greatly increased instability in the commodity markets" (IMF, 1984: 6). However, the percentage of drawings to shortfalls in 1984 fell to 41, and though increasing to 76 per cent in 1985, fell to 55 in 1986 and then rather sharply to 26 and 28 per cent in the following two years.

Table 4.4: Aggregate IMF-CFF drawings in relation to other uses of IMF credit (January 1976 - December 1988)

	Amount			Shares					
				By types of use			By country groups		
	Total	Developed countries[1]	Developing countries	Total	Developed countries[1]	Developing countries	Total	Developed countries[1]	Developing countries
	(Billions of SDRs)			(Per cent)					
Total use of fund credit	64.49	10.48	54.01	100	100	100	100	16	84
CFF	15.61	2.24	13.37	24	21	25	100	14	86
Other facilities [2]	48.88	8.24	40.64	76	79	75	100	17	83

Source: IMF Research Department.

1 Includes industrial countries as defined in the IFS, plus Botswana, Lesotho, South Africa, Swaziland, Greece, Malta, Portugal, Yugoslavia and Israel.
2 Includes credit tranches and extended fund facility, oil facility, and buffer stock financing facility and loans under the "structural adjustment facility" (SAF) and "enhanced structural adjustment facility" (ESAF) in the amount of SDR 0.9 billion in 1986-88.

Table 4.5: Aggregate IMF-CFF drawings as per cent of aggregate shortfalls (January 1976 - August 1989)

	Number of drawings (1)	Drawings (2)	Shortfalls (3)	Drawings as per cent of shortfalls (2)/(3) x 100
		(billions of SDRs)		
1975 Decision	88	3.41	6.86	50
1979 Decision	152	8.43	13.58	62
of which:				
1981	29	1.18	2.41	49
1982	28	2.52	4.03	63
1983	24	2.84	3.78	75
1984	8	0.82	2.01	41
1985	13	0.93	1.22	76
1986	8	0.53	0.97	55
1987	6	1.18	4.53	26
1988	10	0.73	2.65	28
1989 CCFF Decision [1]	4	0.81	2.27	36

Source: IMF (1984), p. 9.

[1] January to August

The IMF Cereal Import Financing Scheme

In May 1981 the Executive Board of the IMF expanded the coverage of the IMF-CFF to include the import of cereals. This established "in conjunction with the IMF's existing compensatory financing facility, a means of providing assistance to members in the financing of temporary increases in the cost of cereal imports that are caused by factors largely beyond a member's control" (IMF, 1981: 84). In addition, the country must have a balance-of-payments need.

Shortfalls in domestic food production or increases in the world prices of cereals will lead to temporary increases in the cost of importing cereals, if domestic food consumption is not to drop. If funds for the increase in the cereal import costs cannot be found, then domestic food consumption will have to be reduced. If this reduction is not possible because of its already low level, then the import of other essential goods will have to be curtailed. The Cereal Decision, as the May 1981 announcement came to be known, would enable a member country to finance its excess cereal imports without decreasing its import of other essential goods. It was expected to make an important contribution to the world food security situation by preventing possible reductions in food consumption, especially in the very poor countries.

As noted in the earlier description of the IMF-CFF, the Cereal Decision provides for the integration of export shortfalls and cereal import excesses as the base for the compensation, which then becomes the algebraic sum of export shortfalls and cereal import excesses. Once the decision is made to have an integrated system, it is binding for three years.

The most important feature of an integrated scheme is the automatic offsetting between the two elements. For example, if there is an export excess in the year when there is a cereal import excess, then the cereal import excess is automatically reduced by the amount of the excess in export earnings. The argument is that the need for help to cover the excess in cereal imports is reduced when there is an excess in export earnings.

The trend in cereal imports, for calculating the excess in cereal imports, is obtained as the average of five years of cereal imports centred on the shortfall year. The average used, unlike that for export earnings, is the arithmetic average.

The scheme permits the estimation of data for up to twelve months. This ensures an extremely quick consideration of any request for compensation so that funds will become available for financing cereal imports when needed. However, if the estimated cereal imports proved to be excessive in relation to actual imports, then the scheme provides for the immediate repurchase of the drawing.

The IMF cereal import financing scheme was established for an initial period of four years, starting in May 1981. In May 1985 it was renewed without change for a further four years. Table 4.6 shows the drawings under the Cereal Decision for the first four years of its operation. Seven countries had made eleven drawings for a total amount of SDR 962.5 million. Malawi made three drawings, South Korea and Bangladesh two each, and Ghana, Morocco, Kenya and Jordan one each.

Of the total drawings of SDR 962.5 million, only SDR 393.8 million were drawn to cope with temporary increases in the cost of importing cereals. The greater part, SDR 568.7 million, was used for compensating shortfalls in export earnings. This seemingly curious phenomenon of the Cereal Decision, producing drawings that have more to do with export shortfalls than cereal import excesses, is explained by the requirement that, once a country decides to have export

Table 4.6: Drawings under the Cereal Decision (millions of SDR)

Country	Date of purchase	End of relevant year	Total		Export component		Cereal component	
			Amount	% of quota	Amount	% of quota	Amount	% of quota
1. Malawi	9/81	6/81	12.0	42.1	0	0	12.0	42.1
2. Korea	1/82	9/81	106.2	41.5	0	0	106.2	41.5
3. Morocco	4/82	3/82	236.4	105.1	113.0	50.3	123.4	54.8
4. Kenya	5/82	12/81	60.4	58.3	28.8	27.8	31.6	30.5
5. Bangladesh	8/82	9/82	71.2	31.2	37.6	16.4	33.6	14.8
6. Malawi (2nd)	2/83	9/82	12.2	42.8	12.2	42.8	0	0
7. Korea (2nd)	6/84	12/83	279.7	60.4	279.7	60.4	0	0
8. Malawi (3rd)	8/84	12/83	13.8	37.0	13.8	37.0	0	0
9. Ghana	12/84	5/84	58.2	28.5	49.2	24.1	9.0	4.4
10. Jordan	1/85	6/84	57.4	77.7	34.4	46.5	23.0	31.1
11. Bangladesh (2nd)	4/85	12/84	55.0	19.1	0	0	55.0	19.1
	Countries	Drawings						
Total	7	11	962.5		568.7		393.8	
Breakdown A								
First Drawings	7	7	601.8		263.0		338.8	
Subsequent Drawings	3	4	360.7		305.7		55.0	
Breakdown B								
Korea, Morocco and Jordan	3	4	679.7		427.1		252.6	
Low-Income Countries	4	7	282.8		141.6		141.2	

Source: Ezekiel (1985), p. 4.2.

shortfalls and cereal import excesses in its compensation base, then it is required to draw under the Cereal Decision for three years even if it had no cereal import excess.

5
IMF-CFF: Impact on Export Instability and Economic Growth

Introduction

From the description of the IMF-CFF and its operations, it is clear that there is quite a sophisticated system for dealing with the compensatory financing of shortfalls in export earnings. It is also clear that it is an operation of some magnitude, as it consumes a quarter of all the credit extended by the IMF, and that it is one of some experience, as it has been running now for nearly a quarter of a century.

In spite of this, the IMF-CFF has been criticized in three areas. The first is that it possesses certain characteristics which might have prevented it from decreasing the export instability of its participating members. The second is that, even if it had succeeded in stabilizing export earnings, it could not provide a permanent solution to the reduction of earnings instability, as it does not attack the causes of export instability at the commodity and country levels. The third is that, by linking the scheme to balance-of-payments considerations, it can theoretically help only a sub-group of those developing countries experiencing export instability. At the same time, the cereal import financing scheme has had only a limited impact on reducing uncertainty in the supply of food in the poorest of the developing countries.

Impact on Export Instability

Finger and Derosa study

The first study available on the effectiveness of the IMF-CFF in reducing the instability of export earnings of its participating members is the one done by Finger and Derosa (1980). This was carried out for a group of seventy-one participating countries over the period 1963-77. They calculated the instability indices for two categories of export earnings: "export earnings with CFF", which is export earnings increased by the CFF compensations in the years in which the funds were actually received and decreased by repayments in the years in which they were actually made, and "export earnings without CFF". Instability is measured by the standard error from regressing the natural logarithm of the variable concerned against time.

The difference between the instability index of "export earnings with CFF" and that of "export earnings without CFF" measures the impact of the CFF on export instability. If the former is smaller than the latter, then the operation of the CFF has been successful in reducing the degree of export instability. If it is larger, then the operation of the CFF would have increased export instability.

The results of this analysis show that the ability of the facility to reduce export instability over the period 1963-77 was very limited. In fact, the operation of the CFF had increased, rather than decreased, the instability of export receipts available to thirty-five of the sixty-two participating developing countries, and to five of the nine participating developed countries. Column (1) of Table 5.1 shows that for the sixty-two developing countries as a whole, export instability was increased by an average of 0.1 per cent. For only eight of these did CFF transactions change export instability by as much as 5 per cent and in five of these the effect was to increase, rather than decrease, export instability. For the nine developed countries as a whole, export instability was increased by an average of 0.3 per cent, and for the total sample of seventy-one countries by an average of 0.1 per cent.

Finger and Derosa identified four features of the IMF-CFF which could have reduced its effectiveness in stabilizing export earnings. The first is the repayment schedule. A member can only make a drawing when there is an export shortfall and a balance-of-payments need. However, it does not have to repay whenever it has an export surplus and a favourable balance-of-payments or reserves position, as there is a grace period of two years, covering the second and the third year after the drawing, and so long as repayment is completed within five years of the drawing. Export instability can be reduced if symmetry was imposed on the conditions for drawing and repayment, and the repayment begins in the year after the drawing if export earnings are good. The country's foreign exchange would be increased by CFF purchases in a bad export year and decreased by CFF repayments in a good export year.

Table 5.1: Effect of IMF-CFF transactions on export instability of participating countries, 1963-77 and 1976-77

(Average percentage decrease (–) and Increase (+) in export instability index)[a]

Number of participating countries	IMF-CFF purchases and repayments, 1963-77		IMF-CFF purchases 1963-77		IMF-CFF adjusted purchases [b] 1976-77
	Actual purchases	Adjusted purchases [b]	Actual purchases	Adjusted purchases [b]	
	(1)	(2)	(3)	(4)	(5)
Developing countries (62)	+0.1	-1.2	-0.2	-1.5	-0.5
Developed countries (9)	+0.3	+0.8	+0.1	+0.6	+4.2
All countries (71)	+0.1	-0.5	-0.1	-0.7	+1.1

Source: Finger and Derosa (1980), p. 16.

a The weight used in calculating the group average was the share of each country in the total export receipts of the group.
b The purchases were adjusted by having them evenly distributed over the actual twelve-month shortfall period.

As there is no symmetry requirement and the interest charged on outstanding drawings is below the market rate, those participating developing countries which have only limited access to the private capital markets would have every incentive to delay the repayments for as long as possible. For such countries, the availability of foreign exchange, rather than its stability, may be more important, and the IMF-CFF funds would be a convenient and cheap source of funds for general development purposes.

The second reason is the formula used for determining *ex ante* when a country has an export shortfall and the size of it. The formula permits the use of provisional data for the shortfall year and whenever these are not available for the use of estimates for up to twelve months. It also uses forecasts for the export earnings of the two post-shortfall years. To obtain accurate forecasts is not easy at the best of times and becomes even more difficult when the exercise is carried out for countries whose export earnings are very unstable to begin with. Most of these countries would not have, *prima facie*, participated in the scheme if their export earnings were stable. If an export shortfall was determined for a year of export surplus and the drawing was made, then the whole exercise would have increased rather than decreased export instability. Even if the direction of change had been forecasted accurately, the size of the export shortfall might have been grossly understated. This would then have produced a drawing whose stabilizing effect would have been minimal.

The third is the administrative time-lag between the occurrence of the export shortfall and the receipt of the borrowing from the facility. If the funds were received a year after the shortfall, they could come at a time when export earnings were on the increase again and produce a destabilizing effect instead.

The fourth is that the size of a country's quota in the IMF and the quota limits imposed on CFF purchases do not allow enough drawings to match the estimated export shortfalls in every case. This would severely limit the ability of the facility, even if it does not suffer from the other deficiencies, to cope adequately with reducing the size of the fluctuations.

The importance of three of the four destabilizing factors mentioned was tested by Finger and Derosa. To eliminate the effect of delay in receiving the funds, the CFF drawing was adjusted by having it evenly distributed over the actual twelve-month shortfall period. For example, if the shortfall period included the last three months in 1966 and the first nine months in 1967, one quarter of the CFF drawing concerned would have been distributed to 1966 and three quarters to

1967. The results given in column (2) of Table 5.1 show that the elimination of the delay in receiving the funds did not increase the ability of the IMF-CFF to reduce export instability. For the sample of developing countries, instability was reduced by only 1.2 per cent on average, and for the sample of developed countries, it was increased by 0.8 per cent. The results given in column (4), when the export earnings were increased by the adjusted CFF purchases only, were more or less the same.

For the sample of seventy-one countries studied by Finger and Derosa over the period 1963-77, the IMF-CFF determined *ex ante* that there were 127 cases where compensational export shortfall existed. In spite of all the facilities at the disposal of the IMF and the participating countries, they were correct in only sixty-two of the cases. Mistakes in forecasting export shortfalls would appear to have been very important in the inability of the facility to reduce export instability significantly. However, it should be noted that this is not a direct test of the importance of inaccurate forecasting in the inability of the facility to stabilize export earnings.

The influence of inadequate drawings was tested by repeating the exercise with the purchases on a distributed basis for the period after the liberalization programme of December 1975, when the funds available were increased very markedly. If inadequate funds had been important in weakening the stabilizing impact of the IMF-CFF, then its stabilizing ability would have been increased considerably after 1975. The results given in column (5) of Table 5.1 show, if anything, that the liberalization had further weakened the stabilizing power of the facility. In the case of developed countries, the increase in export instability, 4.2 per cent, was the highest recorded in the study.

In sum, Finger and Derosa found that the IMF-CFF was unable to reduce export instability significantly over the period 1963-77. They suggested that the inability to forecast export shortfalls accurately was an important reason for this failure, while delays in receiving funds and an inadequate supply of such funds were not important. They did not test for the influence of the asymmetry in the conditions for drawing and repayment.

Herrmann study

Herrmann (1983) examined the stabilizing effect of the IMF-CFF in the export earnings of twenty participating countries over the period 1967-80. The instability indices for export earnings, export earnings plus IMF-CFF payments and less the repayments to it, export earnings plus IMF-CFF payments and export earnings less the repayments to

IMF-CFF were calculated for each of the countries. The instability index was the one proposed by Cuddy and Della Valle (1978).

The operation of the IMF-CFF would have reduced export instability if the instability index of any of the IMF-CFF-adjusted export earnings was smaller than that for the unadjusted export earnings. The instability indices for the three adjusted export earnings and the unadjusted one are given in Table 5.2. The percentage differences between the indices for the adjusted ones, on the one hand, and that for the unadjusted one, on the other, are also given.

When the instability index of export earnings plus IMF-CFF payments, less repayments to it, is compared with that for the unadjusted export earnings, it can be seen that the scheme had been successful in reducing the export instability of only ten of the twenty countries. Moreover, the reduction was not substantial, for in only three countries (Western Samoa, Argentina and Peru) was it more than 5 per cent. In the other ten countries the operation of the scheme had actually increased the level of instability but again the impact was not significant, for in only two cases (Sri Lanka and India) was it greater than 5 per cent.

The stabilizing effect of the IMF-CFF payments on their own was somewhat better as such payments reduced export instability in thirteen of the twenty countries. However, the size of this impact was not significant, as in only four cases (Western Samoa, Argentina, Sudan and Peru) was it greater than 5 per cent. In the other seven countries the impact was destabilizing but again the impact was not great, as in only one case (India) was it greater than 5 per cent.

The stabilizing effect of the scheme is weakest when only the repayments to it are taken into account. In only eight of the twenty cases was a reduction in instability recorded and in only one of these (Guyana) was the reduction greater than 2 per cent. In eleven cases the effect was destabilizing but, as with the earlier comparisons, the impact was not significant: in only two of these (Sri Lanka and Sudan) was the increase in instability greater than 5 per cent.

Of the three adjusted export earnings, the one that is most appropriate in assessing the stabilizing effect of the IMF-CFF is where a country's export earnings are adjusted by adding the IMF-CFF payments and deducting the recipient country's repayments to it. This is because it shows the total effect of the scheme. Adjusting the export earnings by only adding the IMF-CFF payments or deducting the repayments to it will only capture the partial effect. The results from comparing the instability index of the fully adjusted export earnings with that of the totally unadjusted one show that the ability of the

IMF-CFF to reduce export instability over the period 1967-80 was rather limited. This conclusion is supported by those obtained when the export earnings were adjusted only partially. Herrmann's findings are thus consistent with those obtained by Finger and Derosa.

Table 5.2: Effect of IMF-CFF transactions on export instability of participating countries, 1967-80

Country	Instability index[1] (%)				Percentage change between columns:		
	Export earnings	Export earnings + IMF payments – repayments to IMF	Export earnings + IMF payments	Export earnings – repayments to IMF	(2) and (1)	(3) and (1)	(4) and (1)
	(1)	(2)	(3)	(4)	(5)	(6)	(7)
Argentina[2]	21.0	19.7	19.7	20.1	-6.2	-5.9	-0.3
Australia	10.1	10.4	10.3	10.2	2.2	1.5	0.7
Chile	26.3	25.1	25.1	26.4	-4.3	-4.5	0.4
Dominican Republic	18.2	18.6	18.1	18.6	2.0	-0.4	2.1
Egypt	12.8	13.1	13.0	13.0	2.4	1.2	1.2
Guyana	19.0	18.9	19.3	18.6	-0.4	1.4	-2.0
India	10.1	10.9	10.7	10.2	7.7	6.4	1.0
Jamaica	11.5	11.4	11.4	11.6	-0.8	-1.2	0.6
Mexico	29.4	28.3	28.7	29.1	-3.8	-2.6	-1.2
New Zealand	11.3	10.8	10.9	11.2	-4.2	-3.3	-1.2
Peru[2]	25.4	23.9	24.1	25.3	-6.0	-5.4	-0.7
Philippines	15.1	15.1	15.2	15.0	0.0	0.9	-0.7
Sri Lanka	16.2	17.5	15.8	18.0	7.9	-2.3	10.8
South Africa	21.2	20.9	20.9	21.1	-1.4	-1.4	-0.3
South Korea	13.1	13.1	13.0	13.2	0	-0.6	0.2
Sudan	12.2	12.4	11.5	13.1	1.4	-5.6	7.1
Turkey	13.1	13.4	13.4	13.2	1.7	1.6	0.2
Western Samoa	27.8	25.1	25.1	28.0	-9.8	-9.8	0.5
Yugoslavia	9.0	9.0	9.0	9.0	0.0	0.0	0.0
Zambia[2]	26.2	25.3	25.4	26.1	-3.5	-3.1	-0.3

Source: Herrmann (1983), p. 13.

1 The index is the one used by Cuddy and Della Valle (1978).
2 The period analysed is 1966-79.

Further empirical analysis

The analysis by Finger and Derosa was for the first fifteen years of the operation of the IMF-CFF. The results for a more recent period may be different, especially as the method for measuring the trend was changed in 1979 from an arithmetic estimate to a geometric one. Moreover, the terminal years of the periods examined by them may well be exceptional ones. The very sharp increase in the CFF drawings by developing countries in 1976 (SDR 1,520 million, compared to the previous maximum of SDR 300 million in 1972) and the equally sharp increase in the export earnings of non-OPEC developing countries in 1976 and 1977 might have affected the results unduly.

At the same time, there may be technical errors in Finger and Derosa's work. First, the use of the standard error of estimate as the instability index may not be illuminating. Some scaling, for example, by the mean of the relevant series, is needed to avoid the problem that differences in the estimate may arise purely from arbitrary differences in the denomination of the data set used. Second, the trend value for export earnings for all countries was obtained by regressing the natural logarithm of export earnings against time. No explanation was given for the use of such a logarithmic time-trend for all of the countries in the sample. It is possible that the trend values for the export earnings of some countries will be estimated more accurately by the use of a linear function, in which case the estimated trend value and the subsequent instability index would give a wrong picture of the real situation.

In view of the possible weaknesses of the Finger and Derosa study, a further analysis of the impact of the operation of the IMF-CFF on export instability was carried out by Lim (1987b). The period covered was 1963-84. The analysis also deals with two sub-periods, 1963-77 and 1978-84, the first of which coincides with the Finger and Derosa period to provide some comparisons.

The instability index of export earnings adjusted by the IMF-CFF purchases was compared with that of export earnings alone. The index used is the standard error of estimate from regressing the variable concerned against time, normalized by the mean. Both the linear and the logarithmic functions were used. The results are presented in Table 5.3.

When the linear formulation was used for the earlier period, 1963-77, the analysis shows that IMF-CFF purchases had reduced the export instability of only fifteen, or 42.8 per cent, of the sample of thirty-five countries. Moreover, the size of this decrease was very small, averaging only 0.4 per cent. At the same time, the export earnings of ten countries, or 28.6 per cent of the sample, were actually made more unstable, while those of another ten were not affected at all. For the thirty-five countries as a whole, export instability was reduced

Table 5.3: Effect of IMF-CFF purchases on export instability of participating countries, 1963-84

	Countries where IMF-CFF purchases:						Total no. of countries	Unweighted average decrease (–) and increase (+) in export instability (%)		
	Reduced export instability		Increased export instability		Made no difference			Countries experiencing decrease	Countries experiencing increase	All countries
	No.	%	No.	%	No.	%				
Linear time-trend[1]										
1963-77	15	42.8	10	28.6	10	28.6	35	-0.4	0.2	-0.1
1978-84	28	66.7	5	11.9	9	21.4	42	-0.6	0.02	-0.4
1963-84	27	84.4	0	0	5	15.6	32	-0.4	-	-0.3
Logarithmic time-trend[2]										
1963-77	18	51.4	13	37.1	4	11.4	35	-0.9	0.4	-0.3
1978-84	25	59.5	17	40.5	0	0	42	-0.3	0.2	-0.1
1963-84	26	81.2	6	18.8	0	0	32	-0.2	0.2	-0.2

Source: Lim (1987b).

1 The estimating equation is $X = a + bt$, where X is export earnings or export earnings plus IMF-CFF purchases, and t time.
2 The estimating equation is $\log X = a + bt$ where X and t are as defined previously.

by an average of only 0.1 per cent.

When the logarithmic formulation was used for the 1963-77 period, the results were more or less the same. The percentage of the sample which had their export instability reduced was higher at 51.4 per cent. However, the average percentage of this decline in export instability, though higher, was only 0.9 per cent. Moreover, there were relatively more countries, 37.1 per cent, which had their export instability increased. The average decline in instability for the sample as a whole was only 0.3 per cent.

It can be seen that the results obtained by the use of the logarithmic function for 1963-77 are very similar to those obtained by Finger and Derosa (1980) using the same function. They found that the purchases of IMF-CFF reduced export instability by an average of 0.1 per cent for their sample of seventy-one countries, while the Lim (1987b) results show an average decrease of 0.3 per cent for a sample of 35 countries. The results of Finger and Derosa (1980) are also consistent with those obtained by Lim (1987b) using the linear function.

Table 5.3 also shows that the operation of the IMF-CFF had not been successful in stabilizing export revenue over the more recent period of 1978-84. It is true that the percentages of countries with reduced export instability were higher (66.7 per cent with the linear formulation and 59.5 per cent with the logarithmic one). However, the respective averages of these decreases were only 0.6 per cent and 0.3 per cent. For the total sample of forty-two countries, the linear analysis produced an average decline in instability of only 0.4 per cent, the logarithmic analysis one of only 0.1 per cent.

When the entire period, 1963-84, was analysed, both the linear and the logarithmic functions produced a much higher percentage of the sample of thirty-two countries benefiting from the IMF-CFF. In the case of the linear analysis, twenty-seven, or 84.4 per cent, of the thirty-two countries studied had their export instability reduced, and none had its instability increased. However, the average decline for the twenty-seven countries was a mere 0.4 per cent, with that for the sample as a whole even lower at 0.3 per cent. In the case of the logarithmic analysis, twenty-six, or 81.2 per cent, of the sample of thirty-two countries experienced a drop in their instability but only at an average of 0.2 per cent. At the same time six of the countries had their instability increased. The average decrease in instability for the thirty-two countries was only 0.2 per cent.

The results suggest that the operation of the IMF-CFF had not been effective in moderating fluctuations in the export earnings of the participating countries over the period 1963-84. While the analysis shows more countries to have had their export instability reduced when compared to the findings of the Finger and Derosa study, the size of the reduction is insignificant. Thus, in spite of a number of weaknesses, the main conclusion of the Finger and Derosa study for the period 1963-77 still holds for the longer and more recent period, 1963-84. This is that the operation of the IMF-CFF does not significantly reduce fluctuations in the export earnings of the participating countries, the change in the method of forecasting in 1979 notwithstanding. This conclusion holds whether the time-trend used was linear or logarithmic.

The analysis by Lim (1987b) has been updated with an analysis for sixty countries for the period 1963-87. Three time-trends are now used, the linear and the logarithmic ones as in the previous analysis, together with one exponential one. The results are given the Table 5.4.

When the linear time-trend is used, forty-two, or 70 per cent, of the sample of sixty countries had their export instability reduced by the use of IMF-CFF purchases. However, as with the previous analysis, the impact was insignificant, averaging only 0.2 per cent per country. The operation increased the export instability of seventeen countries by an average of 0.4 per cent. For the entire sample, export instability was reduced by an average of 0.1 per cent. Thus, to all intents and purposes, IMF-CFF purchases have had no impact in reducing export fluctuations.

The situation was the same when the logarithmic time-trend was used. The majority of the countries, 76.7 per cent, experienced a decline in instability but the average size of this reduction was very small (0.1 per cent). On the other hand, ten countries had their export instability increased by an average of 1.1 per cent, which is considerably greater than the average decrease, though still insignificant in absolute terms. For the sample as a whole, export fluctuations declined on average by only 0.1 per cent.

The same results were obtained with the use of the exponential time-trend. In conclusion, it can be said that no matter what the period of analysis and no matter what time-trend was used, the results show very clearly that the operation of the IMF-CFF has not significantly reduced the export instability of the participating countries.

Conclusions

The analysis suggests that the so-called judgemental approach used for estimating the export shortfall, in which forecasting for export proceeds in the two post-shortfall years is required, may have to be changed.

Table 5.4: Effect of IMF-CFF purchases on export instability of participating countries, 1963-87

	Countries where IMF-CFF purchases:						Total no. of countries	Unweighted average decrease (–) and increase (+) in export instability (%)		
	Reduced export instability		Increased export instability		Made no difference			Countries experiencing decrease	Countries experiencing increase	All countries
	No.	%	No.	%	No.	%				
Linear time-trend[1]	42	70.0	17	28.3	1	1.7	60	-0.2	+0.4	-0.1
Logarithmic time-trend[2]	46	76.7	10	16.3	4	6.6	60	-0.1	+1.1	-0.1
Exponential time-trend[3]	45	75.0	14	23.3	1	1.7	60	-0.2	+1.2	-0.1

[1] and [2] are as explained in Table 5.3.
[3] The estimating equation is $X = a + bt + ct^2$.

There is already an element of forecasting involved in arriving at export earnings for the shortfall year, for where hard data are not available, provisional data are used, and when this is not available, estimates can be used for up to twelve months. The whole exercise makes the calculation of the export shortfall extremely sensitive to data inaccuracy and forecasting errors.

Given the difficulties and inaccuracies of forecasting, there may be a case for not basing the trend value for estimating the export shortfall on forecasts. If a medium-term trend is required, then an exponential or linear trend value can be obtained by regression analysis using data for, say, the last five years. A longer-term trend may require the use of data for the last seven to ten years. The functional form which gives the better fit should be used.

There is every chance that the value obtained in this way will be more accurate than that obtained by the current method. Even if the results are not better, the use of a known, rather than an "unknown", formula for calculating the trend value enables the potential participating member to know in advance, with more certainty, the amount it can purchase from the facility. This would be an incentive to make greater use of the facility. It is interesting to note that in July 1982, 58 out of 111 developing countries which are members of the IMF, did not have any outstanding drawing from the CFF. Many of these had export shortfalls but did not make any request for drawing, possibly because of the existence of conditionality, that is, the lack of automaticity in drawing rights. This uncertainty would have been increased by that arising from the use of a judgemental approach in arriving at the shortfall estimate.

Another criticism of the existing system that can be raised in this context is the inappropriateness of using nominal values in estimating the shortfall in export earnings. A country with a shortfall in nominal export earnings but not a shortfall in real terms, because of a larger proportionate drop in import prices, requires no compensation. On the other hand, a country with no shortfall in nominal terms but a shortfall in real terms, because of an increase in import prices, requires help (MacBean and Nguyen, 1985).

By providing compensation on the basis of nominal terms, the present system may therefore give help when it is not needed and deny it when it is. In an important sense, this is a more serious weakness than the one observed earlier that the facility cannot stabilize export earnings in nominal terms. Even if nominal export earnings were stabilized, real export earnings might not have been stabilized at the right time. Thus the "real" assistance provided is perverse and is therefore wasteful. There is need for further work here.

The failure to stabilize the nominal or real export earnings of primary producers would therefore imply that the IMF-CFF has not been able to neutralize the deleterious effects of export instability on economic growth.

There is a direct cost too to the primary producers concerned. In a recent and very important contribution to the literature on the microeconomic analysis of commodity price stabilization and the economics of risk, Newbery and Stiglitz (1981) show that a high level of income risk can be very costly to primary producers. These producers' elasticity of marginal utility with respect to income (i.e. the way in which increases in their utility respond to changes in their income) was found to vary between 1.0 and 2.0. With the coefficient of variation of their net income to be between a third and a half, the risk premium can cost between 5 and 25 per cent of their income.

Impact on Causes of Instability

Even if the IMF-CFF had been successful in reducing export instability, it can still be argued that its particular method of dealing with it, through the compensating of export shortfalls, provides no long-term solution to the problem.

The analysis presented early in this study shows that volume instability is more pronounced than price instability at the country level, and that supply factors cannot be ignored in explaining fluctuations in export earnings. This is also the view of Goreux (1980), in a study for the IMF, where he pointed out that at the country level the effect of volume factors is often greater than that of price factors. The causes of volume uncertainty were seen to be supply factors which were specific to the countries concerned, for example, weather conditions, strikes or socio-political factors.

In response to the UNCTAD Expert Group's report on compensatory financing, the IMF (1986) presented data which further supported this view. One set of data has been reworked slightly by UNCTAD and presented as Table 2.1 in this study. This shows that over the period September 1979 to September 1985, volume shortfall was more important than price shortfall in explaining shortfalls in export earnings in seventy-five (or 61 per cent) of the 125 cases. In its response, the World Bank (1986) also agreed with the view that supply instability is a more important factor in commodity export earnings instability than fluctuations of commodity prices.

Volume shortfalls could, in turn, be caused by a drop in domestic supply or a decline in external demand. Of the seventy-five cases where earnings shortfalls were brought about mainly by volume uncertainty, sixty, or 80 per cent of the total, were caused largely by lower export levels. In order to identify the major causes of these sixty supply-oriented volume shortfalls, the most important specific cause for each of the most significant twenty-one commodities is given in Table 5.5. Fifty-four occasions of volume shortfall were recorded and thirty-one, or 57 per cent of these, were due to adverse weather conditions. Drought (15 occasions), hurricane/cyclone damage (8) and heavy rains/floods (4) did the most harm. Other supply factors cited were other natural causes (4 occasions), domestic production problems (9), marketing and transportation difficulties (6), and domestic and international unrest (4). Inclement weather was therefore the major cause of volume shortfall and, not surprisingly, fifteen of the twenty-one commodities identified as being the most susceptible to supply uncertainty were agricultural products.

The statistical information provided by the IMF shows that domestic supply factors are largely responsible for supply instability. This then produces revenue instability which could work through many channels to slow down the rate of economic growth.

The conclusion that revenue instability is caused very significantly by the operation of domestic supply factors would suggest a plan of action which acts directly on these domestic supply constraints. However, the IMF-CFF does not do this. Instead, it provides financial assistance to deal with the adverse consequences of supply inelasticity, and quite deliberately steers clear of any attempt to eliminate the causes of export instability. In line with this, the compensatory financing it offers is of the general fungible type designed only to help with the balance-of-payments difficulties. No attempt is made to ensure that the funds are used to tackle the causes rather than the effects of supply instability.

An approach which deals only with the effects and not the causes of supply instability cannot prevent export instability from recurring. The wisdom of spending a significant part of scarce international development funds on this basis can be questioned as it does not attempt to provide a permanent solution to the problem. This is especially so as the facility has manifestly failed to stabilize export earnings and as there are possible ways of wholly or partly eliminating the causes of supply instability.

Nothing can be done to escape inclement weather but something can be done to reduce its impact. Crop rehabilitation and relocation

Table 5.5: Summary of causes of supply-related volume shortfalls drawings under the IMF-CFF, 1979-85 [1]

Causes	Frequency	Commodities involved
Weather	31	
Drought	15	Cocoa, coconut products, cotton (2), groundnuts and groundnut products (3), tobacco, wheat (2)
Hurricane/cyclone damage	8	Bananas (4), cocoa, coffee, nutmeg, sugar
Heavy rains/flooding	4	Cocoa, coffee, cotton, tea
Other	4	Cocoa, maize, rice, wheat
Other natural causes	4	
Poor fish catches	2	Marine products (2)
Depletion of mineral reserves	1	Copper
Depletion of forestry reserves	1	Forestry products
Domestic problems affecting production	9	
Labour unrest/strikes	5	Bananas, bauxite and aluminium (2), copper, sugar
Shortages of inputs	2	Cocoa, coffee
Disputes between buyers and sellers	1	Beef
Cessation of company operations	1	Shrimp
Marketing and transportation problems	6	
Transportation	5	Coffee, copper, sugar, tobacco (2)
Smuggling	1	Diamonds
Civil unrest and international conflict	4	Cocoa, cotton (2), iron ore
Total	54	

Source: IMF (1986) in UNCTAD (7 April 1986), p. 29.

1 Relates to causes of shortfalls for individual commodities with shortfalls equivalent to at least 25 per cent of the shortfall in total earnings.

programmes, and irrigation and water control projects can do much to mitigate the adverse effects that droughts and heavy rains have on supply. So can the provision of adequate warehouse facilities for storage and improvements in the access to roads and transportation. Traditionally, investment undertaken to ensure the continuity of supply is accorded less priority than that undertaken to increase supply. If this attitude is changed and compensatory financing used to fund the ensuing programmes, then the degree of supply uncertainty caused by the vagaries of the weather can be reduced.

Supply uncertainty can also be caused by uncertainty in the supply and costs of important inputs such as seeds, fertilizers, pesticides, seasonal labour and bank credits. This impact can be reduced if compensatory finance were spent on procurement, stocking and distribution programmes for major inputs, and short-term loan programmes for the purchase of such inputs and for the repair of essential equipment.

None of these programmes to deal with the causes of supply instability is easy to design and implement. However, greater effort and IMF-CFF funds expended on them can yield more lasting results in reducing supply and earnings instability. There is nothing in the IMF-CFF provisions that prevents its compensating finance from being used in this direct way but the approach of the IMF, based as it is on dealing with the effects rather than the causes of supply instability, does not encourage it.

It is important to note that while most of the studies show that supply factors were, on balance, more important than demand factors in explaining export instability at the country level, they did not say that demand factors can be ignored. However, as demand factors have to do basically with uncertainty in the demand for primary products by Western industrial countries, there is little that can be done practically. To all intents and purposes, dealing with the causes of export instability means dealing with the causes of supply instability.

Impact on Economic Growth

Even if the IMF-CFF had been able to reduce the instability of real or nominal export earnings by tackling its causes at the commodity and country levels, it has been argued that its usefulness in reducing the harmful effect of export instability on economic growth is confined to a sub-group of those developing countries experiencing export instability.

Export instability was seen to act against economic growth because it reduces the level and the efficiency of investment through the inflation it encourages, the extra costs it creates, and the precautionary discounting of potential investment returns. These constitute the investment case against export instability and can be presented whether the country concerned suffers from a balance-of-payments deficit or not.

Then there is the administrative case against export and other types of instability. First, the need to constantly monitor and counter changes in the level of foreign exchange has a high opportunity cost in diverting scarce personnel from other more important duties. Second, uncertainty in the receipt of foreign exchange may force the holding of larger international reserves than needed, and third, it may interrupt the import of strategic goods at critical moments in the implementation of development plans. The first two arguments apply even if there is a balance-of-payments surplus, though their impact would be particularly strong with a balance-of-payments deficit. The third operates only when there is a balance-of-payments deficit.

The last case against export instability, that uncertainty in the prices and incomes received by small-scale, landless and poor primary producers can lead to social and political unrest, is not related at all to balance-of-payments considerations.

Thus of the many arguments against export instability, only one is directly related to the balance-of-payments. This is the one which sees it as increasing uncertainty in the import capacity of a country through having an unstable balance-of-payments situation. By giving compensatory financing only when there is a balance-of-payments need, the IMF facility appears therefore to deal only with this issue and to ignore the majority of the arguments against export instability. By further requiring that the export shortfall which brings about the balance-of-payments deficit be temporary, the facility can only be used by countries in periods when their balance-of-payments fluctuate around the "balanced" position (pattern I in Figure 5.1). It cannot be used by countries during periods when their balance-of-payments deficits fluctuate around a declining trend (pattern II). Nor are countries which experience fluctuating balance-of-payments surpluses entitled to make drawings from the facility (pattern III).

In a study of the distribution of forty-eight participating countries in the IMF-CFF by the pattern of their balance-of-payments over the period 1963-84, Lim (1987a) shows that nearly 92 per cent of them were classified under pattern I in the years in which they drew from the facility (Table 5.6). Six per cent were classified under pattern II and 2 per cent under pattern III.

These figures show quite clearly that over the period 1963-84 the IMF-CFF was operated quite strictly in accordance to the guidelines laid down. It was established to deal with temporary balance-of-payments disturbances and was operated as such over the period.

When the analysis was updated to 1987, more or less the same results were obtained. Thus Table 5.6 shows that over the period

Figure 5.1: Patterns of change over time

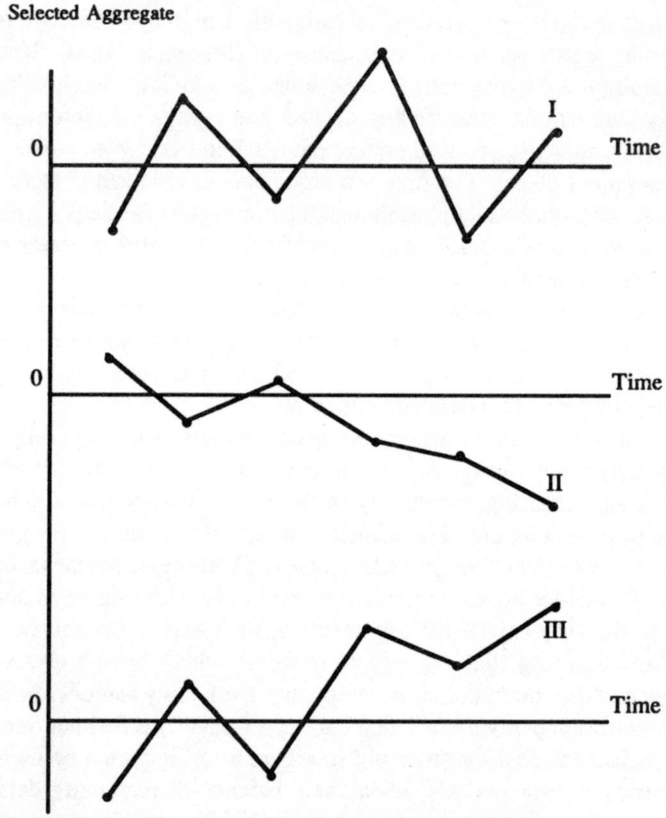

1963-87, 65 per cent of the sixty participating countries had balance-of-payments whose trend resembles pattern I of Figure 5.1. Only 27 per cent of the countries could be classified under pattern II and 8 per cent under pattern III. While the balance in favour of pattern I was significantly less than that over the 1963-84 period, the vast majority of the sixty participating countries in the IMF-CFF had balance-of-payments which fluctuated around the balanced position over the period. Thus over the 1963-87 period, funds from the IMF-CFF were used largely by countries which experienced only temporary disturbances in their balance-of-payments, and were therefore used in the manner intended.

By word and deed, the IMF-CFF thus provides most of its funds to participating countries with balance-of-payments which fluctuate around the "balanced" position. This stance can be supported because countries with other patterns for their balance-of-payments have recourse to other more appropriate facilities of the IMF and to some of the facilities offered by the World Bank. Thus, those countries with consistently worsening balance-of-payments deficits require drastic structural changes, not temporizing at the margin. The economic adjustment programme of the IMF and the structural adjustment loan programme of the World Bank would be more appropriate. Similarly those countries with fluctuating but healthy balance-of-payments surpluses can do much by themselves to reduce the other adverse effects of export instability. There seems little justification for using scarce international development funds on such countries. Thus, while the evidence shows that funds from the IMF-CFF were used for only a sub-group of those developing countries experiencing export instability, the reason for such a selective use of the funds is economically sound. In any case, the sub-group benefiting from the funding is a large one, having accounted for 92 per cent and 65 per cent of the participating countries over the 1963-84 and 1963-87 periods respectively.

Table 5.6: Distribution of participating countries in IMF-CFF by pattern of change for selected aggregates, 1963-84 and 1963-87.

Variable	Pattern[1]	Number of countries		% distribution of countries	
		1963-84	1963-87	1963-84	1963-87
Balance-of-payments	I	44	39	91.7	65.0
	II	3	16	6.2	26.7
	III	1	5	2.1	8.3
	Total	48	60	100.0	100.0
Current account	I	11	20	22.9	33.3
	II	37	36	77.1	60.0
	III	0	4	0	6.7
	Total	48	60	100.0	100.0
Merchandise trade	I	19	15	39.6	25.0
	II	25	34	52.1	56.7
	III	4	11	8.3	18.3
	Total	48	60	100.0	100.0

[1] The pattern of change is obtained by fitting $Y = a + bT$, where Y is the selected aggregate and T the time variable. The results for 1963-87 are given in Appendices 5.1, 5.2 and 5.3

It can also be pointed out that the percentage distribution of the participating countries by the three patterns is very different if the aggregate used is the balance on the current account. Table 5.6 shows that 77 per cent of the forty-eight countries for the 1963-84 period were grouped under pattern II and only 23 per cent under pattern I. This means that the majority of the countries drawing from the IMF-CFF did so in periods when their current account was in deficit. When the aggregate used is the merchandise trade account, the predominance of pattern II was reduced but still remained at 52 per cent, which is significantly higher than the 40 per cent recorded for pattern I cases. Interestingly, pattern III cases account for a not insignificant 8 per cent of the observations: countries received help even when they experienced, on the whole, rising current account surpluses.

More or less the same picture appears when the analysis is for the longer 1963-87 period. When the current account aggregate was used, 60 per cent of the sixty countries appeared under pattern II and only 33 per cent under pattern I. While the difference is not as dramatic as that over the 1963-84 period, it was still very significant and shows that the majority of the countries drew from the fund when they had a long-term deficit in their current account. Table 5.6 also shows that nearly 7 per cent of the participating countries had a long-term surplus in their current account.

When the merchandise trade account was used, pattern II countries retained their dominant position (57 per cent) as recipients of IMF-CFF funds. Pattern I countries made up only 25 per cent of the sample while the share of pattern III went up to over 18 per cent.

These figures show that the use of different aggregates produces different results on the range of developing countries drawing from the IMF-CFF. They do not support the contention that the facility would only come to the help of those countries experiencing temporary shortfalls in their export performances. Countries which experienced secular declines in their current account and merchandise trade had been granted assistance as had, though on a much smaller scale, countries with secular increases in those aggregates.

They also show that the distribution of IMF-CFF funds between the three patterns of change is more even when the variables used are the current account and the merchandise trade account. A third important observation is that countries experiencing a long-term decline in their current account and their merchandise trade account overtook countries experiencing neither long-term decline nor long-term surplus in these variables, as the major recipients of IMF-CFF funds.

On balance, there does not appear much to the argument that the usefulness of the IMF-CFF is limited to a sub-group of those developing countries experiencing export instability. When the balance-of-payments aggregate is used, the vast majority of the participating countries had deviations in this aggregate around the "balanced" position. However, such countries are the ones to assist, for those with unstable but declining balance-of-payments deficits require help of another kind, while those with unstable but increasing balance-of-payments surpluses do not require external help. When the balance of current account or of merchandise trade is used, the majority of the countries assisted had secularly declining trends. The IMF-CFF should then be accused of being over-generous and not mean in its operations.

Impact on Food Security

Low level of drawings

The expectation that the IMF cereal import financing facility would provide funds on an important scale to developing countries for financing temporary increases in their foodgrain imports has not been fulfilled. Over the first four years of its operation, May 1981 to May 1985, drawings totaled only SDR 962.5 million, and of this sum only SDR 393.8 million were drawn to fund temporary increases in the cost of importing cereals.

These sums were dwarfed in comparison to the shortfalls in cereal production over the period. Table 5.7 show that these shortfalls were even greater than those recorded in the world food crisis of 1973-75. The shortfalls were in Africa, and in particular sub-Saharan Africa, and in Latin America.

Of the seven countries which did make use of the IMF cereal import financing facility, South Korea, Morocco and Jordan could not be said to be low-income, food-deficit countries. Their total drawings equaled SDR 679.7 million, or 70.6 per cent of the total, while their drawings under the cereal component was SDR 252.6 million or 64.1 per cent of the amount made under that vote. Thus the low-income and food-deficit countries of Bangladesh, Ghana, Kenya and Malawi played only a minor role in a very small group of countries that made use of the facility.

These results hardly show that the facility had made much inroad in increasing the certainty of food supply in the most needy countries. Also, it could not have increased the certainty of supply of other essential imports. As a mechanism then for increasing the

Table 5.7: Shortfalls in cereal production,[1] 1973-75 and 1981-83

	1973	1974	1975	3-year Average	1981	1982	1983	3-year average
				(thousand metric tons)				
ASIA								
Number of countries	1	4	3		4	8	5	
Shortfalls	25.4	11560.5	1277.3	4287.7	264.4	9550.4	1057.2	3624.0
- excluding India	25.4	613.1	1277.3	638.6	264.4	1059.7	1057.2	793.8
AFRICA								
Number of countries	17	10	9		16	16	20	
Shortfalls	1623.4	1370.1	724.3	1239.3	902.2	2142.0	3259.1	2101.1
LATIN AMERICA								
Number of countries	3	4	2		0	1	3	
Shortfalls	57.3	88.9	31.4	59.2	0	123.4	365.9	163.1
TOTAL								
Number of countries	21	18	14		20	25	28	
Shortfalls	1706.1	13019.4	2033.0	5586.2	1166.6	11815.8	4682.2	5888.2
- excluding India	1706.1	2072.1	2033.0	1937.1	1166.6	3325.0	4682.2	3057.9

Source: Ezekiel (1985), p. 2.5.

1 Shortfalls equal the difference between actual and trend production. Data for China (P.R.), Maldives and St. Vincent are not included.

availability of cereals, it could not be said to have been successful as the drawings were relatively small. This is especially the case as far as the impact on the poorest of the developing countries was concerned. As a result, its power to stabilize the availability of cereals and of essential imports was limited. Thus the use of the facility as a mechanism for dealing with the adverse effect of instability in cereal availability on economic growth would appear to be small.

Reasons for low level of drawings

An important reason for the low level of drawings under the Cereal Decision might have been the lack of a need for it. The African countries with shortfalls in cereal production would have been helped by food aid. As the world foodgrain prices in 1981-83 were not as high as those in 1974-75, part of the shortfall could have been made up by purchases on the world market.

Ezekiel (1985) claimed that the features of the facility might have been more important. The effect of the requirement for a balance-of-payments need and the use of an integrated base for compensation might have been particularly severe. A country may have an export surplus and a shortfall in the production of cereals at the same time, but not a balance-of-payments deficit. If the export surplus had led to an increase in the imported inputs required for producing the export goods, then there will be no spare foreign exchange to pay for any import of cereals. As there is not an overall balance-of-payments deficit, the country cannot draw from the IMF cereal import financing facility, even though there is a desperate need for it.

The point is that economic and institutional conditions within a country do not always allow for the extra foreign exchange earned from an export surplus to be used for financing a cereal import excess. The automatic offsetting mechanism implied in the use of an integrated base for calculating compensation does not always work. If there is no balance-of-payments deficit, then the existence of the IMF facility is of no consequence, even though there may be a great need for cereal imports.

The trend in cereal imports, used for calculating the excess in cereal imports, is measured by the arithmetic average of five years' cereal imports centred on the shortfall year. Using this calculation, as the period of the cereal import excess lengthens, the excess, and hence the amount that can be drawn from the facility, diminishes (Goreux, 1980; Ezekiel, 1985). As food crises in poor countries tend to last for a number of years in succession, the effect would be to reduce the amount of assistance they can obtain from the facility.

The quota constraint system may also be effective in limiting the level of drawings. At the moment the separate quota constraint is 83 per cent each for the cereal component and the export component, while the joint quota constraint is 105 per cent of the quota. The size of the joint quota constraint means that the separate quota constraint for cereals could drop from 83 per cent to 22 per cent of the quota (105 per cent less 83 per cent). This is a very low permissible level in view of the severity and duration of food crises in developing countries.

The provisions for repayments may also deter countries from drawing from the facility. A grace period of two years follows the year the drawing is made. Repayments, in equal quarterly instalments, begin in the fourth year and must be completed by the end of the fifth year, regardless of the economic conditions prevailing in those years. It is possible that these may turn out to be bad years in which case the consumption of cereals may have to be reduced in order to finish making the repayments. This is a risk that some countries may not be prepared to take.

The requirement of co-operation, especially for requests in the upper tranche when evidence of adequate co-operation is needed, may be another deterrent. Countries may be tempted to ask why a temporary increase in the cost of importing cereals should be tied to policy adjustment programmes. By definition, the phenomenon is temporary and requires no corrective measure.

Testing for importance of reasons

Ezekiel (1985) carried out some tests to support the claim that the features of the facility were more important than exogenous factors in explaining the low level of drawings. For 1981, thirteen of the thirty-eight countries studied had export shortfalls, totalling SDR 377.6 million. Of the thirteen, only ten could have drawn under the export component for a sum of SDR 215.9 million. Sixteen countries had excess cereal imports totalling SDR 649.6 million. Only eight of them could have drawn under the cereal component for a sum of SDR 57.9 million. The difference between the actual and the compensatable export shortfalls or excess cereal imports was due to the use of the constraint, imposed by the integration principle, that no country with a zero value for net shortfall (the algebraic sum of export shortfall and cereal import excess) can be compensated.

The results of the operation of the integration principle on drawings are striking. They show eight of the thirty-eight countries studied could have been compensated under the Cereal Decision for a total of SDR 119.4 million, with SDR 57.9 million for cereal import excesses and SDR 61.5 million for export shortfalls. These are considerably smaller than the respective estimates of the funds needed. The use of the integrated base for compensation could thus explain the actual limited drawing shown in Table 4.6.

Although the facility did not come into operation until 1981, the same exercise was carried out by Ezekiel for 1973-75 in order to test the influence of the much higher world cereal prices in that period on the level of the drawings. As in the case of the analysis for 1981, the figures of export shortfalls and cereal import excesses were actual rather than the projected ones used by the IMF-CFF.

The exercise shows that in 1975, twenty-nine countries were compensated for excesses in cereal imports to the tune of SDR 563.2 million, compared to the eight countries with a sum of SDR 57.9 million in 1981. This suggests that the higher world cereal prices did increase the drawings in 1975. An equally important result is that the cereal import excesses in 1975 amounted to SDR 792.7 million. While the gap in 1975 between the total of the cereal import excesses and the compensatable sum was relatively smaller than that in 1981, it was still significant and shows the operation of the integration principle at work in restricting the size of the potential drawings.

Conclusions

Contrary to the impression given, Ezekiel did not set out to test the importance of each of the facility's characteristics in limiting the level of drawings for cereal import excesses. All that was done was to show that the use of an integrated base for the compensation had a critical limiting effect. However, this is not a surprising result because the resources set aside for the compensation of export shortfalls and cereal import excesses is small in relation to the sum required.

The impact of even this rather mechanical result is reduced by the fact that the effect of the availability of food aid on the demand for cereal import financing is not examined. World cereal prices in 1981-84 were lower than they were in 1975 because of the surplus of foodgrain in the developed countries. This same surplus would have encouraged the greater supply of food aid, which would have reduced the need for assistance from the IMF cereal import financing scheme.

A test was carried out on the effect of the lower cereal prices in 1981-84 on the demand for assistance from the IMF. It was found that more countries were compensated and the funds committed were, in nominal terms, larger in 1975 than in 1981. From this was concluded that the lower foodgrain prices in 1981-84 had decreased the demand for help from the IMF. This is a rather indirect and unsatisfactory test. Other factors could have been more important and their influence, as well as that of price, could have been tested more directly. Also, it would have been useful to know the extent of the price influence, if it had in fact operated.

In spite of these weaknesses, the Ezekiel study has produced an important conclusion. If food security is seen to be of paramount importance, its attainment can be more realistically achieved by not asking for more funding for the compensatory financing scheme operating under the integration principle. A better solution may be to have the same level of funding, but to discard the integration principle, with more emphasis given to the cereal component, because of the special importance of food in the development process. For the first period of its operation, 1981-84, the IMF cereal import financing scheme appears to have played only a small role because the funds available to cereal import excesses *per se* were limited and the food-deficit developing countries had access to other sources of food supply.

Appendix 5.1: Pattern of Balance-of-Payments (Y) Over Time (T) 1963-87: Y = a + bT

Country	a	b	$\bar{R}^2$	F-ratio
Argentina	2.9705e+5	-150.79	0.232	8.25
	(2.87)	(-2.87)		
Australia	1.0802e+5	54.88	0.016	1.40
	(-1.18)	(1.18)		
Bangladesh	-2.4717e+4	12.47	0.052	1.76
	(-1.33)	(1.33)		
Barbados	-4.1179e+2	0.21	-0.034	0.31
	(-0.56)	(0.56)		
Bolivia	3.9802e+4	-20.21	0.566	32.28
	(5.66)	(-5.68)		
Cameroon	1.436e+3	-0.73	-0.062	0.06
	(0.25)	(-0.25)		
Central African Rep.	1.5853e+3	-0.80	0.088	2.74
	(1.65)	(-1.65)		
Chad	7.2409e+2	-0.37	-0.035	0.36
	(0.60)	(-0.60)		
Chile	1.9167e+5	-97.32	0.280	10.34
	(3.21)	(-3.22)		
Congo	2.2892e+4	-11.59	0.231	5.50
	(2.34)	(-2.35)		
Costa Rica	4.5940e+4	-23.33	0.625	41.01
	(6.39)	(-6.40)		
Cyprus	5.8101e+3	2.96	0.139	4.88
	(-2.20)	(2.21)		
Dominican Republic	1.0583e+4	-5.38	0.027	1.64
	(1.28)	(-1.28)		
Egypt	-7.0028e+3	3.44	-0.043	0.02
	(-0.15)	(0.15)		
Fiji	1.1742e+3	-0.59	-0.015	0.67
	(0.82)	(-0.82)		
Gambia	7.6074e+2	-0.39	-0.050	0.19
	(0.44)	(-0.44)		
Greece	1.3612e+4	-6.82	-0.035	0.22
	(0.47)	(-0.47)		
Guyana	1.7451e+4	-8.87	0.544	27.19
	(5.20)	(-5.22)		
Iceland	-2.3569e+3	1.20	0.006	1.15
	(-1.07)	(1.07)		
India	4.4300e+4	-22.40	-0.023	0.49
	(0.70)	(-0.70)		
Israel	-4.0039e+4	20.37	0.064	2.63
	(-1.62)	(1.62)		

(continued over)

Appendix 5.1 (continued)

Country	a	b	$\bar{R}^2$	F-ratio
Ivory Coast	2.2802e+4	-11.59	0.067	2.57
	(1.60)	(-1.60)		
Jamaica	6.7945e+3	-3.46	-0.006	0.86
	(0.92)	(-0.93)		
Kenya	5.6831e+3	-2.89	-0.018	0.58
	(0.76)	(-0.76)		
Korea	-5.5622e+4	28.33	0.098	3.60
	(-1.89)	(1.90)		
Malawi	2.6973e+3	-1.37	0.048	2.17
	(1.47)	(-1.47)		
Malaysia	-7.2457e+4	36.82	0.312	11.86
	(-3.431)	(3.44)		
Mali	3.1136e+4	-15.72	0.024	1.51
	(1.23)	(-1.23)		
Mauritania	3.6609e+3	-1.86	0.090	2.59
	(1.60)	(-1.61)		
Mauritius	-1.7321e+3	0.87	-0.038	0.17
	(-0.41)	(0.41)		
Mexico	1.2537e+5	-63.71	-0.016	0.63
	(0.79)	(-0.79)		
Morocco	4.639e+3	-2.37	-0.033	0.23
	(0.47)	(-0.48)		
Nepal	6.4674e+3	-3.26	-0.015	0.83
	(0.91)	(-0.91)		
New Zealand	2.6823e+5	-136.15	0.809	85.60
	(9.22)	(-9.25)		
Nicaragua	4.7529e+4	-24.14	0.601	35.59
	(5.95)	(-5.97)		
Pakistan	3.1125e+4	-15.84	0.057	2.21
	(1.48)	(-1.49)		
Panama	5.678e+3	-2.88	0.196	6.60
	(2.56)	(-2.57)		
Papua New Guinea	1.0687e+4	-5.38	-0.009	0.90
	(0.95)	(-0.95)		
Peru	1.5198e+5	-77.17	0.448	20.51
	(4.52)	(-4.53)		
Philippines	2.3707e+4	-12.01	-0.033	0.24
	(0.49)	(-0.49)		
Portugal	-1.3268e+5	67.04	0.147	3.59
	(-1.89)	(1.90)		
Romania	-4.0987e+3	2.03	-0.071	0.01
	(-0.09)	(0.08)		

(continued over)

Appendix 5.1 (continued)

Country	a	b	$\bar{R}^2$	F-ratio
Senegal	8.240e+3	-4.18	0.291	7.57
	(2.74)	(-2.75)		
Sierra Leone	1.2938e+4	-6.57	0.518	25.75
	(5.06)	(-5.08)		
South Africa	-2.951e+3	1.48	-0.043	0.01
	(-0.08)	(0.08)		
Spain	-5.0855e+4	25.98	-0.035	0.23
	(-0.47)	(0.47)		
Sri Lanka	2.5466e+3	-1.30	-0.035	0.20
	(0.44)	(-0.44)		
Sudan	3.1962e+4	-16.26	0.437	19.60
	(4.41)	(-4.43)		
Tanzania	9.899e+3	-5.04	-0.018	0.59
	(0.77)	(-0.77)		
Thailand	1.8568e+4	9.46	0.021	1.51
	(-1.22)	(1.23)		
Togo	-6.8292e+2	0.35	-0.038	0.19
	(-0.43)	(0.43)		
Tunisia	9.2538e+2	-0.46	-0.042	0.04
	(0.20)	(-0.20)		
Turkey	6.3046e+4	-32.13	0.047	2.19
	(1.47)	(-1.48)		
Uganda	5.4766e+3	-2.79	0.050	2.11
	(1.44)	(-1.45)		
Uruguay	-4.5563e+3	2.31	-0.024	0.44
	(-0.66)	(0.66)		
Western Samoa	-5.4764e+2	0.28	0.168	5.44
	(-2.33)	(2.33)		
Yemen PDR	4.163e+3	-2.11	0.104	3.33
	(1.82)	(-1.82)		
Zaire	6.4242e+4	-32.65	0.555	29.68
	(5.43)	(5.45)		
Zambia	2.5376e+4	-12.90	0.187	6.06
	(2.45)	(-2.46)		
Zimbabwe	-6.9521e+3	3.51	-0.093	0.15
	(-0.38)	(0.38)		

Appendix 5.2: Pattern of Current Account (Y) Over Time (T) 1963-87: Y = a + bT

Country	a	b	$\bar{R}^2$	F-ratio
Argentina	3.0522e+5	-155.00	0.375	15.42
	(3.92)	(-3.93)		
Australia	8.4206e+5	-428.13	0.787	93.292
	(9.62)	(-9.66)		
Bangladesh	2.0925e+4	-10.80	-0.039	0.47
	(0.67)	(-0.69)		
Barbados	-1.0044e+3	0.49	-0.039	0.22
	(-0.49)	(0.47)		
Bolivia	3.1974e+4	-16.25	0.481	23.26
	(4.80)	(-4.82)		
Cameroon	6.6446e+5	-33.71	0.700	38.31
	(6.17)	(-6.19)		
Central African Rep.	5.5683e+3	-2.83	0.482	17.72
	(4.19)	(-4.21)		
Chad	3.2665e+3	-1.65	0.038	1.75
	(1.32)	(-1.32)		
Chile	1.7976e+5	-91.43	0.363	14.70
	(3.82)	(-3.83)		
Congo	3.2442e+4	-16.49	0.076	2.24
	(1.49)	(-1.50)		
Costa Rica	3.2582e+4	-16.60	0.483	23.42
	(4.81)	(-4.84)		
Cyprus	1.2341e+4	-6.28	0.243	8.71
	(2.93)	(-2.95)		
Dominican Republic	2.7219e+4	-13.87	0.318	12.18
	(3.47)	(-3.49)		
Egypt	1.4036e+5	-71.54	0.396	16.74
	(4.07)	(-4.09)		
Fiji	2.8448e+3	-1.46	0.022	1.50
	(1.21)	(-1.23)		
Gambia	6.8045e+2	-0.35	-0.057	0.08
	(0.28)	(-0.28)		
Greece	1.9593e+5	-99.76	0.706	56.10
	(7.45)	(7.49)		
Guyana	1.3682e+4	-6.96	0.63	37.80
	(6.12)	(-6.15)		
Iceland	3.1945e+3	-1.64	-0.022	0.48
	(0.68)	(-0.69)		
India	1.3947e+5	-71.02	0.046	2.12
	(1.45)	(-1.45)		
Israel	4.5795e+4	-23.48	-0.001	0.99
	(0.98)	(-0.99)		

(continued over)

Appendix 5.2 (continued)

Country	a	b	$\bar{R}^2$	F-ratio
Ivory Coast	7.4615e+4	-37.98	0.202	6.56
	(2.55)	(-2.56)		
Jamaica	1.9196e+4	-9.79	0.224	7.91
	(2.79)	(2.81)		
Kenya	3.3426e+4	-17.02	0.231	8.22
	(2.85)	(-2.87)		
Korea	-9.1293e+4	45.93	-0.029	0.32
	(-0.57)	(0.57)		
Malawi	7.4248e+3	-3.79	0.080	2.99
	(1.71)	(-1.73)		
Malaysia	8.5423e+4	-43.43	0.021	1.52
	(1.23)	(-1.23)		
Mali	1.1968e+4	-6.09	0.654	40.76
	(6.35)	(-6.38)		
Mauritania	2.4220e+4	-12.29	0.612	26.24
	(5.10)	(-5.12)		
Mauritius	2.7982e+3	-1.43	-0.019	0.58
	(0.75)	(-0.76)		
Mexico	6.7686e+4	-35.13	-0.039	0.10
	(0.31)	(-0.31)		
Morocco	1.0339e+5	-52.65	0.250	9.01
	(2.99)	(-3.00)		
Nepal	2.8307e+4	-14.32	0.807	47.01
	(6.84)	(-6.86)		
New Zealand	1.6740e+5	-85.09	0.630	34.80
	(5.87)	(-5.90)		
Nicaragua	5.8622e+4	-29.80	0.592	34.32
	(5.84)	(-5.86)		
Pakistan	4.3945e+4	-22.56	0.119	3.70
	(1.90)	(-1.92)		
Panama	-2.0837e+4	10.54	0.120	4.28
	(-2.07)	(2.07)		
Papua New Guinea	6.8516e+4	-34.68	0.469	14.22
	(3.76)	(-3.77)		
Peru	8.0794e+4	-41.15	0.176	6.13
	(2.46)	(-2.48)		
Philippines	1.0130e+5	-51.54	0.080	3.07
	(1.74)	(-1.75)		
Portugal	-4.0159e+4	19.98	-0.064	0.10
	(-0.32)	(0.31)		
Romania	-1.9562e+5	98.88	0.114	2.92
	(-1.71)	(1.71)		

(continued over)

Appendix 5.2 (continued)

Country	a	b	$\bar{R}^2$	F-ratio
Senegal	4.6235e+4	-23.48	0.683	35.51
	(5.94)	(-5.96)		
Sierra Leone	6.0523e+3	-3.09	0.121	4.18
	(2.03)	(-2.04)		
South Africa	-1.2793e+5	64.77	0.012	1.30
	(-1.14)	(1.14)		
Spain	1.6566e+4	-8.79	-0.045	0.01
	(0.11)	(-0.12)		
Sri Lanka	3.5740e+4	-18.18	0.385	16.03
	(3.99)	(-4.00)		
Sudan	1.1413e+4	-5.84	0.027	1.66
	(1.27)	(-1.29)		
Tanzania	2.8594e+4	-14.55	0.436	18.81
	(4.32)	(-4.34)		
Thailand	1.5189e+5	-77.28	0.347	13.77
	(3.69)	(-3.71)		
Togo	9.4585e+3	-4.81	0.153	4.97
	(2.22)	(-2.23)		
Tunisia	4.8040e+4	-24.46	0.485	23.56
	(4.83)	(-4.85)		
Turkey	1.7446e+5	-88.80	0.363	14.69
	(3.81)	(-3.83)		
Uganda	3.2114e+3	-1.6324	-0.019	0.61
	(0.78)	(-0.78)		
Uruguay	2.1570e+4	-10.98	0.163	5.66
	(2.37)	(-2.38)		
Western Samoa	-6.8627e+1	0.03	-0.047	0.02
	(-0.14)	(0.13)		
Yemen PDR	1.8577e+4	-9.44	0.583	28.90
	(5.35)	(-5.38)		
Zaire	4.4863e+4	-22.86	0.146	4.93
	(2.21)	(-2.22)		
Zambia	4.7554e+4	-24.15	0.314	11.54
	(3.39)	(-3.40)		
Zimbabwe	-1.3731e+4	6.82	-0.104	0.06
	(-0.25)	(0.25)		

Appendix 5.3: Pattern of Merchandise Trade Balance (Y) Over Time (T) 1963-87: Y = a + bT

Country	a	b	$\bar{R}^2$	F-ratio
Argentina	-2.3622e+5	120.23	0.329	12.75
	(-3.55)	(3.57)		
Australia	1.3279e+5	-67.12	0.094	3.58
	(1.90)	(-1.89)		
Bangladesh	1.4470e+5	-73.62	0.600	22.00
	(4.66)	(-4.69)		
Barbados	3.0317e+4	-15.43	0.856	125.73
	(11.15)	(-11.21)		
Bolivia	-1.993e+4	6.11	0.481	23.26
	(-1.65)	(1.66)		
Cameroon	-5.0227e+4	25.46	0.518	18.18
	(-4.25)	(4.26)		
Central African Rep.	5.6447e+3	-2.86	0.594	25.87
	(5.07)	(-5.09)		
Chad	6.9480e+3	-3.53	0.225	6.52
	(2.54)	(-2.55)		
Chile	-2.0570e+4	10.47	-0.032	0.25
	(-0.50)	(0.50)		
Congo	-7.6181e+4	38.60	0.631	26.61
	(-5.15)	(5.16)		
Costa Rica	5.0797e+3	-2.61	-0.005	0.88
	(0.92)	(-0.94)		
Cyprus	6.6180e+4	-33.67	0.893	201.78
	(14.137)	(-14.21)		
Dominican Republic	5.7569e+4	-29.25	0.735	67.54
	(8.19)	(-8.22)		
Egypt	4.4043e+5	-224.01	0.87	160.23
	(12.60)	(-12.66)		
Fiji	1.5255e+4	-7.77	0.501	23.11
	(4.78)	(-4.81)		
Gambia	3.2248e+3	-1.64	0.029	1.50
	(1.22)	(-1.23)		
Greece	4.7504e+5	-241.91	0.873	159.15
	(12.54)	(-12.62)		
Guyana	-3.1262e+3	-1.58	0.112	3.76
	(1.94)	(-1.94)		
Iceland	-1.2725e+3	0.63	-0.036	0.16
	(-0.41)	(0.40)		
India	4.4958e+5	-228.59	0.488	22.89
	(4.77)	(-4.78)		
Israel	1.9147e+5	-97.93	0.164	5.70
	(2.37)	(-2.39)		

(continued over)

Appendix 5.3 (continued)

Country	a	b	$\bar{R}^2$	F-ratio
Ivory Coast	-9.5790e+4	48.72	0.660	45.59
	(-6.72)	(6.75)		
Jamaica	2.9299e+4	-14.91	0.468	22.07
	(4.67)	(-4.70)		
Kenya	5.2690e+4	-26.82	0.429	19.05
	(4.34)	(-4.37)		
Korea	-1.0486e+5	52.78	-0.017	0.59
	(-0.77)	(0.77)		
Malawi	-6.4484e+3	3.26	0.161	5.40
	(-2.33)	(2.32)		
Malaysia	-2.8188e+5	143.31	0.426	18.81
	(-4.32)	(4.34)		
Mali	9.867e+3	-5.02	0.538	25.42
	(5.01)	(-5.04)		
Mauritania	7.5629e+3	-3.85	0.020	1.320
	(1.14)	(-1.14)		
Mauritius	4.3219e+3	-2.20	0.064	2.57
	(1.59)	(-1.60)		
Mexico	-7.4674e+5	378.65	0.279	10.26
	(-3.20)	(3.20)		
Morocco	1.4944e+5	-76.01	0.721	62.89
	(7.89)	(7.931)		
Nepal	5.1100e+4	-25.90	0.777	39.27
	(6.24)	(-6.27)		
New Zealand	-1.0753e+4	5.49	-0.046	0.12
	(-0.35)	(0.35)		
Nicaragua	4.0196e+4	-20.42	0.476	20.96
	(4.56)	(-4.58)		
Pakistan	3.4634e+5	-176.03	0.795	78.41
	(8.81)	(-8.86)		
Panama	6.2383e+4	-31.80	0.832	120.18
	(10.89)	(-10.96)		
Papua New Guinea	2.1678e+4	-10.95	0.064	2.03
	(1.42)	(-1.42)		
Peru	-1.9989e+4	10.17	-0.027	0.37
	(-0.60)	(0.61)		
Philippines	1.1262e+5	-57.32	0.153	5.34
	(2.30)	(-2.31)		
Portugal	2.1098e+5	-107.81	0.101	2.69
	(1.62)	(-1.64)		
Romania	-3.3717e+5	170.58	0.338	8.13
	(2.85)	(2.85)		

(continued over)

Appendix 5.3 (continued)

Country	a	b	$\bar{R}^2$	F-ratio
Senegal	4.4404e+4	-22.57	0.617	26.73
	(5.15)	(-5.17)		
Sierra Leone	6.7434e+3	-3.43	0.160	5.39
	(2.31)	(-2.32)		
South Africa	-4.9333e+5	250.68	0.385	15.99
	(-3.99)	(4.00)		
Spain	6.3968e+5	-326.33	0.514	25.29
	(4.99)	(-5.03)		
Sri Lanka	5.7368e+4	-29.16	0.550	30.32
	(5.49)	(-5.51)		
Sudan	3.4648e+4	-17.61	0.341	13.42
	(3.65)	(-3.66)		
Tanzania	5.7995e+4	-29.48	0.797	91.27
	(9.52)	(-9.55)		
Thailand	1.1356e+5	-57.86	0.270	9.88
	(3.12)	(-3.14)		
Togo	6.8213e+3	-3.47	0.119	3.98
	(1.99)	(-2.00)		
Tunisia	9.9537e+4	-50.66	0.770	81.45
	(8.98)	(-9.03)		
Turkey	3.4767e+5	-176.95	0.717	61.81
	(7.82)	(-7.86)		
Uganda	4.1737e+3	-2.09	-0.014	0.72
	(0.86)	(-0.85)		
Uruguay	-5.0694e+3	2.57	-0.035	0.18
	(-0.43)	(0.43)		
Western Samoa	3.813e+3	-1.94	0.727	59.44
	(7.67)	(-7.71)		
Yemen PDR	6.3365e+4	-32.21	0.743	58.94
	(7.64)	(-7.68)		
Zaire	-4.2475e+4	21.63	0.166	5.56
	(-2.34)	(2.36)		
Zambia	1.2420e+3	-6.15	-0.004	0.90
	(0.97)	(-0.95)		
Zimbabwe	-2.2110e+4	11.23	-0.052	0.50
	(-0.70)	(0.71)		

6
Stabex: Description of its Operations

Aims of Stabex

Stabex was established in 1975 as part of the first Lomé Convention (Lomé I), a co-operation treaty between the European Economic Community (EEC) and forty-six African, Caribbean and Pacific (ACP) countries for the period 1975-79. The second Lomé Convention (Lomé II) was signed in 1979 for the period 1980-84 and the third Lomé Convention (Lomé III) in 1984 for the period 1985-89. Stabex was retained in both of these two later Lomé Conventions. Its aims in the three conventions remain basically the same and have been expressed by Lomé III (article 147) in the following way:

> With the aim of remedying the harmful effect of the instability of export earnings and to help the ACP states overcome one of the main obstacles to the stability, profitability and sustained growth of their economies, to support their development efforts and to enable them in this way to ensure economic and social progress for their peoples by helping to safeguard their purchasing power, a system shall be operated to guarantee the stabilization of export earnings ..... derived from the ACP states' exports to the community or other destinations ..... of products on which their economies are dependent and which are affected by fluctuations in price or quantity or both these factors.

All the three Lomé Conventions thus assume explicitly that export instability is harmful to economic growth. They do not say why this is the case, but the reasons are spelt out in a 1981 report by the Commission of the European Communities (1981) on the operation of Stabex under Lomé I. Instability is said to make investment planning difficult and to disrupt the import of capital goods. It also leads to a reduction in the incomes of primary producers as they are taxed more in order to maintain public expenditure in the face of falling tax revenue resulting from declining export earnings. Such a negative policy on primary producers will lead to a drop in primary production and, hence, in economic growth in the long run.

Stabex seeks to mitigate these adverse effects of instability on growth by stabilizing the proceeds that the ACP countries receive by exporting to the EEC. Stabex is thus not a price stabilization scheme as it provides compensatory financing for shortfalls in export earnings and not for shortfalls in the prices or in the quantities exported. As a result, it is designed not to have any effect on the prices and the quantities of the products exported.

An amount equal to 375 million European Unit of Account (Eua), the EEC's unit of account in 1975, was set aside for operating Stabex under Lomé I. Until the US dollar was floated in 1971, the Eua had the same value as the US dollar. After that, its value has been determined according to the weighted value of the basket of the EEC's national currencies. In 1975 when Lomé I began, the Eua was worth US$1.29. By the start of Lomé II in 1980, the EEC's unit of account was renamed the European Currency Unit (Ecu) and was worth US$1.39. At the beginning of Lomé III in 1985 the value of the Ecu had gone down to US$0.73.

This amount of 375 million Ecu made up 10 per cent of the direct financial contributions from the EEC member states to the European Development Fund (EDF), which was set up under Lomé I for the development of the ACP countries. In Lomé II Stabex received 557 million Ecu, or 10 per cent of the EDF and under Lomé III it was 925 million Ecu, or 10.9 per cent of the EDF.

The scheme is managed by the Commission of the European Communities. However, questions of major importance, such as changing the status of an ACP country and adding or deleting to the list of eligible products, are dealt with jointly by the ACP/EEC Council of Ministers.

The fund allocated for Stabex under each Lomé Convention is divided into five instalments, one for each of the five years of application. For each of these years the resources available consist of the annual instalment of the Stabex fund and the amount replenished for the ACP countries. If these resources are inadequate for a given year of application, the ACP/EEC Council of Ministers can decide to use in advance, up to a maximum of 25 per cent, the following year's instalment or to reduce the amount of the transfers to be made. If the resources available for any one year are not all used the balance will be carried over to the following year.

Stabex allows the ACP countries to apply for transfers in the foreign exchange of their choice. Most of the transfers have been in French Francs, Deutschmarks and Sterling. The choice of the currencies is clearly influenced by the colonial history of the recipient countries and by their current geographical trading pattern.

Rules of Operation

In pursuing its aim to mitigate the adverse economic effects of export instability by guaranteeing the stabilization of export earnings, Stabex has a number of operational rules. These define the operation of the scheme in its attempt to fulfil a very ambitious objective. The most important of these are concerned with its geographical and product coverage, the qualifying criteria for transfers and the repayment system.

Coverage

Stabex is a regional scheme whose membership is limited to the EEC member states, on the one side, and the ACP countries, on the other. The EEC member states provide the funds for operating Stabex and only the ACP countries are allowed to draw from it. In its coverage Stabex is thus different from the compensatory financing facility operated by the International Monetary Fund (IMF-CFF) in two important respects.

First, it does not have a global geographical coverage. Second, it permits only the developing members to apply for transfers, whereas the IMF-CFF allows, in principle, all members to draw from it. In reality most of the drawing countries in the IMF-CFF are developing ones, but countries such as Australia, New Zealand, Greece, Iceland, Romania and Spain have received compensatory financing.

When Stabex was established in 1975 there were eight EEC countries and forty-six ACP ones. In 1979, at the signing of Lomé II, there were nine EEC countries and fifty-eight ACP ones, and by Lomé III the numbers had grown to ten and sixty-six respectively.

Stabex is also unlike the IMF-CFF in that it is a commodity-specific compensatory financing scheme, where shortfalls are calculated on a "gross", that is, commodity-by-commodity, basis.

This means that compensatory payment can be made to a commodity experiencing a shortfall in its export earnings, even if the earnings from other commodities, whether or not in the Stabex list, are buoyant. This makes Stabex a more generous scheme than the IMF-CFF which adopts a "net" balance-of-payments approach. Stabex does allow the aggregating of the shortfalls of the export earnings of certain products belonging to the same family. Examples of product-groups include groundnut products, cocoa products, coffee products, cotton products, coconut products, palm and palmnut products, raw hides and skins and leather, and wool products. However, this provision is introduced to make it easier, and not harder, for some ACP countries to qualify for Stabex funding, as will be shown later in the discussion on qualifying criteria.

Table 6.1 shows the list of eligible products negotiated in the three Lomé Conventions. It also includes the products added as a result of decisions taken by the ACP-EEC Council of Ministers. The products are mainly agricultural raw materials, with some processed agricultural goods, rough timber and fisheries products included. Iron ore was included in Lomé I but was taken out of Lomé II and Lomé III. It is now, together with copper, phosphates, manganese, bauxite, alumina and tin, in the EEC's special financing facility for mining products, Sysmin. However, Sysmin does not offer the same type of financial compensation for shortfalls in export earnings as Stabex.

Four agricultural products which feature very prominently in the exports of some ACP countries have never been covered by Stabex. These are tobacco, sugar, beef and citrus fruits. Sugar and beef have been granted specific preferential arrangements under the Lomé Conventions, but these have little to do with instability issues. Tobacco and citrus fruits have been left out because of domestic protectionist pressures within the EEC. The ACP signatory which has been particularly affected by these exclusions is Malawi which is very dependent on the exports of tobacco.

Stabex is a regional scheme also in the sense that it applies only to the exports of the ACP countries to the EEC. However, the agreement allows for two instances in which this rule may be waived by the ACP-EEC Council of Ministers. The first is when certain ACP countries expressly request for their exports to other ACP countries to be taken into account. The second is when certain ACP countries which export very little to the EEC request that the losses from earnings from their exports to all destinations be covered.

The exports have to originate in the ACP countries and to be released for home use in the EEC or benefit under the inward processing

Table 6.1: Eligible Stabex products in the three Lomé Conventions, 1975-89

	Products originally under Lomé I	NIMEXE Code
1.	Groundnuts, shelled or not	12.01-31 to 12.01-35
2.	Groundnut oil	15.01-74 and 15.07-87
3.	Cocoa beans	18.01-00
4.	Cocoa paste	18.03-10 to 18.03-30
5.	Cocoa butter	18.04-00
6.	Raw or roasted coffee	09.01-11 to 09.01-17
7.	Extracts, essence or concentrates of coffee	21.02-11 to 21.02-15
8.	Cotton, not carded or combed	55.01-10 to 55.01-90
9.	Cotton linters	55.02-10 to 55.02-90
10.	Coconuts	08.01-71 to 08.01-75
11.	Copra	12.01-42
12.	Coconut oil	15.07-29, 15.07-77 and 15.07-92
13.	Palm oil	15.07-19, 15.07-61 and 15.07-63
14.	Palm nut and kernel oil	15.07-31, 15.07-78 and 15.07-93
15.	Palm nuts and kernels	12.01-44
16.	Raw hides and skins	41.01-11 to 41.01-95
17.	Bovine cattle leather	41.02-05 to 41.02-98
18.	Sheep and lamb skin leather	41.03-10 to 41.03-99
19.	Goat and kid skin leather	41.04-10 to 41.04-99
20.	Wood in the rough	44.03-20 to 44.03-99
21.	Wood roughly squared or half-squared, but not further manufactured	44.04-20 to 44.04-98
22.	Wood sawn lengthwise, but not further prepared	44.05-10 to 44.05-79
23.	Fresh bananas	08.01-31
24.	Tea	09.02-10 to 09.02-90
25.	Raw sisal	57.04-10
25a.	Iron ore (ores, concentrates, and roasted iron pyrites)	26.01-12 to 26.01-18
Products added during Lomé I		
26.	Vanilla	09.05-00
27.	Cloves - whole fruit, cloves and stems	09.07-00
28.	Sheep's or lamb's wool, not carded or combed	53.01-10 to 53.01-40
29.	Fine animal hair of Angora goats - mohair	53.02-95
30.	Gum arabic	13.02-91
31.	Pyrethrum - flowers, leaves, stems, peel and roots; saps and extracts from pyrethrum	12.07-10 and 13.03-15

(continued over)

Table 6.1 (continued)

Products added under Lomé I		**NIMEXE Code**
32.	Essential oils, not terpeneless, of cloves, of niaouli and of ylang-ylang	33.01-23
33.	Sesame seed	12.01-68
34.	Cashew nuts and kernels	08.01-77
35.	Pepper	09.04-11 and 09.04-70
Products added by Lomé II		
36.	Shrimps and prawns	03.03-43
37.	Squid	03.03-68
38.	Cotton seeds	12.01-66
39.	Oil-cake	23.04-01 to 23.04-99
40.	Rubber	40.01-20 to 40.01-60
41.	Peas	07.01-41 to 07.01-43 07.05-21 and 07.05-61
42.	Beans	07.01-45 to 07.01-47 07.05-25 and 07.05-65
43.	Lentils	07.05-30 and 07.05-70
Products added during Lomé II		
44.	Nutmeg and mace	09.08-13, 09.08-16, 09.08-60 and 09.08-70
45.	Shea nuts	12.01-70
Products added by Lomé III		
46.	Shea nut oil	ex 15.07-82 and ex 15.07-98
47.	Mangoes	ex 08.01-99
48.	Dried bananas	08.01-35II

arrangements in the EEC in order to be processed.

Qualifying criteria

A number of criteria have to be met before an ACP country can qualify for Stabex funding. The first is the dependency threshold. Under Lomé III, for the product or product-group concerned, the total exports to all, and not just EEC, destinations from the ACP country requesting the Stabex transfer must have brought in earnings that exceed 6 per cent of its total earnings from merchandise exports, during the year preceding the year in question. There are two exceptions to this rule. For sisal the dependency threshold is 4.5 per cent. For the least developed, landlocked and island ACP countries it is 1.5 per cent.

The levels of these dependency thresholds have been reduced over time. In Lomé I, it was 7.5 per cent for the normal product or product-group, 5.0 per cent for sisal and 2.5 per cent for the least developed, landlocked and island ACP countries. In Lomé II, the respective figures were 6.5 per cent, 5 per cent and 2 per cent.

The second qualifying criterion is that the fluctuation threshold must be met. This states that an ACP country may request a transfer of funds if, during a calendar year, its actual earnings from exporting any of the products or product-groups, considered individually, to the EEC are at least 6 per cent below the reference level set for that product or product-groups in the ACP country. For the least developed, landlocked and island ACP countries the fluctuation threshold is much lower at 1.5 per cent of the reference level.

The reference level itself is calculated for each product or product-group for each ACP country. It corresponds to the average of export earnings in the four years preceding the year of application. In cases where the ACP country begins exporting a processed product which has been traditionally exported in its raw form or begins exporting a product which it has not traditionally produced, the average is calculated on the basis of three, instead of four, years preceding the year of application.

The third qualifying criterion is that the shortfall in export earnings to the EEC is not due to trade policies pursued by the ACP country. Another criterion, imposed in Lomé II but not in Lomé III, is that the recorded earnings of the ACP country from its exports to all destinations during the year of application must not exceed the average of its export earnings to all destinations in the four years preceding the year of application.

There are other qualifying criteria but the ones mentioned are the most important. If the criteria are satisfied, then the ACP country's request for a Stabex transfer will be accepted by the Commission of the European Communities, which manages Stabex, and a transfer decision adopted. This decision allows the transfer to be made quickly and also for the payment of advances, both of which will be made available free of interest charges.

The size of the transfer will be equal to the difference between the reference level and the actual export earnings, plus 2 per cent (1 per cent in Lomé I and Lomé II) for statistical errors and omissions. The export statistics used for calculating the qualifying thresholds have to be chosen by the ACP country from either those obtained by cross-checking the statistics of the EEC and the ACP country or those obtained by multiplying the unit values for the exports of the ACP country, as given in that country's statistics, by the quantities imported by the EEC, as shown in the EEC's statistics. The calculations are carried out in Ecu and in nominal terms.

Repayments
Stabex has been established as a revolving fund. With the exception of the least developed ones, ACP countries which have received its funds are, under certain conditions, obliged to contribute towards the replenishment of Stabex's resources during the seven years following the transfer.

The first of these conditions is that the unit value of the product which gave rise to a transfer was higher than the average unit value calculated during the preceding four years. The second is that the quantity of the same product exported to the EEC was at least equal to the average of the quantities exported to the EEC during the preceding four years. The third is that the earnings from exporting the product concerned were equal to at least 106 per cent of the average export earnings for the preceding four years.

If these three conditions are met simultaneously, then the ACP country has to repay an amount equal to the difference between the actual earnings derived in the preceding year from exports to the EEC and the average of export earnings in the preceding four years. However, the repayment cannot exceed the value of the transfer in question.

This amount is to be paid at the rate of one fifth per year after a deferment period of two years. In Lomé III the repayment may be made either direct to Stabex or by deduction from the ACP country's transfer rights or by payment in the ACP country's local currency. In the last case, the ACP country's repayment will be used to cover the local expenditure incurred in European Development Fund-financed projects in the ACP country.

A Hypothetical Transfer

A hypothetical request for a Stabex transfer under Lomé II will be worked through in order to see how the various rules of operation are brought into play.

The ACP country concerned, country X, is not a least developed, landlocked or island country and has to repay the transfer. It exports three major commodities, of which only one, coffee, is an eligible Stabex product.

In January 1982, country X requested a transfer of Ecu 5 million because of a shortfall in the earnings of its coffee exports to the EEC in the previous calendar year. However, it enjoyed a healthy balance-of-payments surplus because its revenue from other exports had increased markedly because of a sharp rise in their prices. The request was for the transfer to be in French Francs.

The Commission of the European Communities, which manages Stabex, had to establish whether country X had satisfied four major qualifying criteria and, if it had, whether the amount requested could be granted. In its investigation the Commission found that the first criterion, the dependency threshold, had been met. Country X's exports of coffee to all countries exceeded 6.5 per cent of its total earnings from its merchandise exports in 1980.

It also found that the second criterion, the fluctuation threshold, had been satisfied. In 1981 its revenue from exporting coffee was 6 per cent below the average of country X's revenue from coffee exports in the period 1977-80, the so-called reference level.

The qualifying criterion that the shortfall in the revenue from exporting coffee to the EEC must not be caused by trade policies pursued by country X was clearly satisfied. The shortfall was due to a fall in the price of coffee brought about by a drop in world demand.

The fourth criterion, that country X's recorded total revenue from exporting to all countries in 1981, was less than the average for the period 1977-80, was also met.

The calculations carried out were based on statistics chosen by country X, as were calculations on the size of the transfer, which was the difference between the reference level and the actual export earnings from coffee in 1981, plus 1 per cent to cover statistical errors and omissions. As country X had done its sums properly the request for a transfer of Ecu 5 million was granted.

It should be noted that the request was granted in spite of the fact that country X had a healthy balance-of-payments surplus in 1981. This is because Stabex operates on a "gross" or commodity-by-commodity basis, unlike the IMF-CFF.

The transfer of Ecu 5 million was free of interest charges and was made twelve months later in January 1983. It had to be repaid over the following seven years (1983-89), provided that three conditions were fulfilled simultaneously. The first was that at the beginning of each of the seven years (e.g. in 1984), the price of coffee in the preceding year (i.e. 1983) exceeded the average for the previous four years (i.e. 1978-82). Using the same years as examples, the second condition was that the volume of coffee exported by country X to the EEC in 1983 must equal the average volume exported over the period 1978-82. The third was that the export revenue from coffee in 1983 averaged 106.5 per cent of the average export revenue for the period 1978-82.

The repayment would be equal to the difference between the actual revenue derived from exporting coffee to the EEC in the preceding year and the average of the revenue over the previous four years. This amount, which could not exceed Ecu 5 million, was to be repaid in equal instalments over five years after a grace period of two years; that is, it was to begin in 1985.

As far as the use of the Stabex transfer was concerned, the first reference to it (article 23) stated that it must be for maintaining financial flows in the coffee sector. However, the same article went on to soften this requirement by saying that the transfer could also be used in other appropriate sectors in order to promote diversification. In its application country X said that it would use the funds for agricultural diversification. This was accepted.

Actual Stabex Transfers

During the period of Lomé I, 1975-79, Stabex had generally enough funds every year to cope with the requests by the ACP countries for transfers. Table 6.2 shows that Ecu 389.9 million were disbursed, Ecu 12.3 million of which went to EEC overseas dependencies which became independent during the period of Lomé I. It can be seen that most of the recipients were African countries and that these accounted for 95 per cent of the total value of the transfers. The biggest beneficiaries were Senegal (16.7 per cent), Sudan (10.7 per cent) and Mauritania (9.5 per cent). An amount equal to Ecu 263 million, or 67.5 per cent of the total transfers, did not have to be reimbursed formally as they went to the least developed, landlocked and island ACP countries.

Table 6.3 shows that under Lomé I the most important triggering products were, by far, groundnuts and groundnut products (35.7 per cent). Iron ore (15.8 per cent), cotton (11.1 per cent) and wood in the rough (10.0 per cent) came next, some distance behind.

The main reason for shortfalls in the export earnings of the triggering products and therefore for claims on Stabex transfers under Lomé I was falling production and not falling prices from a drop in world demand.

The situation under Lomé II was very different. First, the legitimate claims for compensatory financing exceeded the funds available, especially in the first two years. Shortfalls in export earnings in 1980 led to claims in 1981 which totalled Ecu 261 million. Even after resorting to various methods to raise the Stabex funding ceiling for that year, the transfers only amounted to Ecu

Table 6.2: Gross Stabex transfers by country by descending size of loan, 1975-87

Country	Lomé I 1975-79 Ecu m	%	Country	Lomé II 1980-84 Ecu m	%
Senegal	65.11	16.70	Ivory Coast	93.42	13.96
Sudan*	41.78	10.72	Senegal	90.58	13.53
Mauritania*	37.00	9.49	Ghana	85.47	12.77
Niger*	22.65	5.81	Papua New Guinea	50.69	7.57
Tanzania*	20.70	5.31	Kenya	44.87	6.70
Uganda*	20.60	5.28	Sudan*	40.70	6.08
Benin*	20.37	5.23	Cameroon	29.59	4.42
Ivory Coast	15.00	3.85	Togo*	28.83	4.31
Ethiopia*	14.42	3.70	Tanzania*	20.86	3.12
Swaziland*	13.22	3.39	Gambia*	18.15	2.71
Guinea-Bissau*	11.29	2.90	Sierra Leone	14.35	2.14
Mali*	9.78	2.51	Burundi*	13.81	2.06
Central African Republic*	7.83	2.01	Ethiopia*	11.30	1.69
Liberia	7.59	1.95	Mali*	10.70	1.60
Gambia*	7.51	1.93	Madagascar	9.99	1.49
Congo	7.36	1.89	Rwanda*	9.33	1.39
Chad*	7.34	1.88	Vanuatu	8.93	1.33
Burkina Faso*	7.26	1.86	Swaziland*	8.19	1.22
Gabon	6.70	1.72	Sao Tome	7.60	1.14
Madagascar	5.75	1.48	Chad	6.64	0.99
Ghana	5.18	1.33	Comoros*	6.57	0.98
Cameroon	4.06	1.04	Western Samoa*	6.49	0.97
Sierra Leone	3.98	1.02	Central African Republic*	5.20	0.78
Togo*	3.63	0.93	Malawi	4.93	0.74
Dominica*	2.89	0.74	Benin*	4.65	0.69
Western Samoa*	2.84	0.73	Solomon Islands	4.34	0.65
Comoros*	2.33	0.60	Jamaica	4.30	0.64
Kiribati	2.28	0.58	Tonga*	4.01	0.60
Solomon Islands	2.17	0.56	Grenada	3.96	0.59
Fiji	2.11	0.54	Guinea-Bissau*	3.65	0.55
Somalia*	1.93	0.50	Somalia*	3.58	0.53
Burundi*	1.49	0.38	Dominica*	3.53	0.53
Vanuatu	1.43	0.37	Fiji	3.00	0.45
Cape Verde*	1.21	0.31	St Lucia	1.62	0.24
Tonga*	1.21	0.31	Kiribati	1.60	0.24
Djibouti*	0.69	0.18	Lesotho	1.29	0.19
Rwanda*	0.61	0.16	Burkina Faso*	1.05	0.16
Belize*	0.34	0.09	St Vincent	0.91	0.14
Tuvalu*	0.17	0.04	Cape Verde*	0.53	0.08
Lesotho	0.00	0.00	Tuvalu*	0.14	0.02
Jamaica	0.00	0.00			

(continued over)

Table 6.2 (continued)

Country	Lomé I 1975-79 Ecu m	%	Country	Lomé II 1980-84 Ecu m	%
Kenya	0.00	0.00	Gabon	0.00	0.00
St Lucia	0.00	0.00	Djibouti*	0.00	0.00
Papua New Guinea	0.00	0.00	Congo	0.00	0.00
			Belize*	0.00	0.00
G Equatorial	0.00	0.00	Mozambique	0.00	0.00
Mozambique	0.00	0.00	Liberia	0.00	0.00
Malawi	0.00	0.00	Mauritius	0.00	0.00
Sao Tome	0.00	0.00	Mauritania*	0.00	0.00
St Vincent	0.00	0.00	Niger*	0.00	0.00
Mauritius	0.00	0.00	Uganda*	0.00	0.00
Grenada	0.00	0.00	G Equatorial	0.00	0.00
Total	389.81	100.00	Total	669.35	100.00

Country	Lomé III 1985-87 Ecu m	%	Country	1975-87 Ecu m	%
Ivory Coast	179.03	19.45	Ivory Coast	287.45	14.52
Senegal	105.96	11.51	Senegal	261.65	13.22
Ethiopia*	91.61	9.95	Sudan*	146.40	7.40
Papua New Guinea	84.49	9.18	Papua New Guinea	135.18	6.83
Sudan*	63.93	6.95	Ethiopia*	117.33	5.93
Cameroon	60.35	6.56	Cameroon	94.01	4.75
Kenya	40.69	4.42	Ghana	90.65	4.58
Chad*	33.37	3.63	Kenya	85.56	4.32
Solomon Islands	27.70	3.01	Tanzania*	50.47	2.55
Rwanda*	25.36	2.76	Chad*	47.35	2.39
Burundi*	24.52	2.66	Togo*	45.98	2.32
Mozambique	21.45	2.33	Burundi*	39.82	2.01
Central African Republic	18.97	2.06	Mauritania*	37.00	1.87
			Gambia*	36.61	1.85
Vanuatu	16.44	1.79	Mali*	36.05	1.82
Mali*	15.56	1.69	Benin*	35.42	1.79
Togo*	13.52	1.47	Rwanda*	35.30	1.78
Malawi	11.94	1.30	Solomon Islands	34.21	1.73
Gambia*	10.95	1.19	Central African Republic	31.99	1.62
Benin*	10.41	1.13			
Tanzania*	8.91	0.97	Niger*	29.26	1.48
Western Samoa*	7.92	0.86	Vanuatu	26.80	1.35
Burkina Faso*	7.32	0.80	Mozambique	21.45	1.08
Comoros*	7.06	0.77	Swaziland*	21.41	1.08

(continued over)

Table 6.2 (continued)

Country	Lomé III 1985-87		Country	1975-87	
	Ecu m	%		Ecu m	%
Niger*	6.61	0.72	Uganda	20.60	1.04
Madagascar	4.51	0.49	Madagascar	20.24	1.02
G Equatorial	4.51	0.49	Sierra Leone	18.33	0.93
Lesotho	3.14	0.34	Guinea-Bissau*	17.82	0.90
Mauritius	2.95	0.32	Western Samoa*	17.25	0.87
Guinea-Bissau*	2.88	0.31	Malawi	16.87	0.85
Tonga*	2.78	0.30	Comoros*	15.96	0.81
Kiribati	2.46	0.27	Burkina Faso*	15.63	0.79
Sao Tome	1.63	0.18	Sao Tome	9.23	0.47
Grenada	0.97	0.11	Tonga*	8.00	0.40
Fiji	0.26	0.03	Liberia	7.59	0.38
Tuvalu*	0.12	0.01	Congo	7.36	0.37
Sierra Leone	0.00	0.00	Gabon	6.70	0.34
Swaziland*	0.00	0.00	Dominica*	6.43	0.32
Dominica*	0.00	0.00	Kiribati	6.34	0.32
Gabon	0.00	0.00	Somalia*	5.51	0.28
Djibouti*	0.00	0.00	Fiji	5.38	0.27
Somalia*	0.00	0.00	Grenada	4.93	0.25
Congo	0.00	0.00	G Equatorial	4.51	0.23
St Lucia	0.00	0.00	Lesotho	4.43	0.22
Mauritania*	0.00	0.00	Jamaica	4.30	0.22
Ghana	0.00	0.00	Mauritius	2.95	0.15
Liberia	0.00	0.00	Cape Verde*	1.73	0.09
Jamaica	0.00	0.00	St Lucia	1.62	0.08
Belize*	0.00	0.00	St Vincent	0.91	0.05
St Vincent	0.00	0.00	Djibouti*	0.69	0.03
Uganda*	0.00	0.00	Tuvalu*	0.43	0.02
Cape Verde*	0.00	0.00	Belize*	0.34	0.02
Total	920.28	100.00	Total	1979.43	100.00

Note: * Least developed, landlocked and island countries.

158 million. The claims in 1982, for export shortfalls in 1981, came to Ecu 453 million, but only Ecu 142 million of that could be met.

Second, most of the claims for Stabex transfers were the result of declining prices, which was particularly marked for coffee, cocoa and groundnuts. For example, in 1982 coffee triggered off the largest amount of claims as the result of a severe drop in its price in 1981. In the case of Ivory Coast alone this produced a claim of Ecu 99 million. Likewise, falls in the price of cocoa in 1981 resulted in a claim of Ecu 83 million by Ghana alone in 1982. Similarly large decreases in the

Table 6.3: Stabex disbursements by product by descending size of disbursements, 1975-87

Lomé I 1975-79 Product	Ecu m	%	Lomé II 1980-84 Product	Ecu m	%	Lomé III 1985-87 Product	Ecu m	%	1975-87 Product	Ecu m	%
Groundnut products	139.36	35.75	Coffee	246.58	36.84	Coffee	281.35	30.68	Coffee	542.43	27.40
Iron ore	61.79	15.85	Cocoa	148.84	22.24	Groundnut products	163.08	17.78	Groundnut products	435.69	22.01
Cotton	43.36	11.12	Groundnut products	133.26	19.91	Timber	90.96	9.92	Cocoa	212.08	10.71
Timber	39.99	10.26	Cotton	36.53	5.46	Copra/ coconut	85.97	9.37	Cotton	142.53	7.20
Sisal	20.58	5.28	Copra/ coconut	31.63	4.72	Palm oil products	64.96	7.08	Timber	131.35	6.64
Oil cake	17.59	4.51	Bananas	14.22	2.12	Cotton	62.64	6.83	Copra/ coconut	128.17	6.48
Coffee	14.49	3.72	Oil cake	13.99	2.09	Cocoa	61.72	6.73	Palm oil products	79.47	4.01
Copra/ coconut	10.57	2.71	Sisal	9.07	1.35	Tea	35.57	3.88	Iron ore	61.79	3.12
Raw hides & skins	9.09	2.33	Palm oil products	6.71	1.00	Oil cake	20.63	2.25	Oil cake	52.22	2.64
Tea	8.38	2.15	Vanilla	5.16	0.77	Beans	19.19	2.09	Tea	46.20	2.33
Palm oil products	7.80	2.00	Beans	5.00	0.75	Cloves	9.95	1.08	Sisal	33.12	1.67
Bananas	5.81	1.49	Cashews & nuts	4.90	0.73	Cashews & nuts	7.62	0.83	Beans	24.18	1.22
Vanilla	2.90	0.74	Sesame	3.15	0.47	Fats	5.82	0.63	Bananas	20.03	1.01
Sesame	2.63	0.68	Tea	2.25	0.34	Sisal	3.47	0.38	Cloves	13.10	0.66
Cloves	2.30	0.59	Fats	1.94	0.29	Vanilla	1.73	0.19	Cashews & nuts	12.52	0.63
Cocoa	1.52	0.39	Ylang-ylang	1.34	0.20	Raw hides & skins	1.13	0.12	Raw hides & skins	11.14	0.56
Gum arabic	0.85	0.22	Wool	1.29	0.19						

(continued over)

Table 6.3 (continued)

Lomé I			Lomé II			Lomé III					
	1975-79			1980-84			1985-87			1975-87	
Product	Ecu m	%	Product	Ecu m	%	Product	Ecu m	%	Product	Ecu m	%
Pyrethrum	0.61	0.16	Raw hides &			Sesame	0.96	0.10	Vanilla	9.80	0.49
Ylang-ylang	0.17	0.04	skins	0.91	0.14	Prawns	0.39	0.04	Fats	7.76	0.39
Wool	0.00	0.00	Cloves	0.85	0.13	Bananas	0.00	0.00	Sesame	6.74	0.34
Beans	0.00	0.00	Prawns	0.71	0.11	Gum arabic	0.00	0.00	Wool	4.43	0.22
Prawns	0.00	0.00	Nutmeg	0.64	0.10	Wool	0.00	0.00	Ylang-ylang	1.51	0.08
Cashews &	0.00	0.00	Timber	0.39	0.06	Iron ore	0.00	0.00	Prawns	1.10	0.06
nuts	0.00	0.00	Gum arabic	0.00	0.00	Ylang-ylang	0.00	0.00	Gum arabic	0.85	0.04
Nutmeg	0.00	0.00	Iron ore	0.00	0.00	Nutmeg	0.00	0.00	Nutmeg	0.64	0.03
Fats	0.00	0.00	Pyrethrum	0.00	0.00	Pyrethrum	0.00	0.00	Pyrethrum	0.61	0.03
Total	389.80	100.00	Total	669.35	100.00	Total	917.12	100.00	Total	1979.44	100.00

price of groundnuts in 1981 made it an important triggering product in 1982. In Senegal alone this produced a claim of Ecu 63 million. Not surprisingly, the main triggering products in Lomé II were coffee (36.8 per cent of the gross Stabex transfers), cocoa (22.2 per cent) and groundnut products (19.9 per cent).

The geographical distribution of Stabex transfers under Lomé II, also given in Table 6.2 , shows that African countries continued to be the main recipients. The most important of these were the Ivory Coast (13.9 per cent), Senegal (13.5 per cent), Ghana (12.8 per cent), Kenya (6.7 per cent) and Sudan (6.1 per cent). The only non-African recipient of note was Papua New Guinea, which accounted for 7.6 per cent of the funds.

As with Lomé I, most of the recipients were least developed, landlocked and island countries exempted from repayment. However, the percentage of the gross Stabex transfers of Ecu 669.36 million which was exempted was much lower at 31.7 per cent, compared to the 67.5 per cent exemption level in Lomé I.

Table 6.2 shows that in the first three years of Lomé III, from 1985 to 1987, the leading three recipients were the Ivory Coast (19.4 per cent), Senegal (11.5 per cent) and Ethiopia (10.0 per cent). They were followed by Papua New Guinea (9.2 per cent), Sudan (6.9 per cent) and Cameroon (6.6 per cent). By far the most important triggering product was coffee (30.7 per cent), followed some distance behind by groundnut products (17.8 per cent), timber (9.9 per cent), and copra and coconut products (9.4 per cent).

If the share of the ten leading recipient countries in the gross Stabex transfers is taken as the country-concentration of Stabex funding, then Table 6.2 shows that the distribution of the transfers is very uneven and has become more uneven over time. Under Lomé I the share was 69.5 per cent, but under Lomé II it had increased to 75.2 per cent and over the first three years of Lomé III, it had increased further to 77.4 per cent. Over the period 1975-87 the Ivory Coast (14.5 per cent) and Senegal (13.2 per cent) were the most important recipients, followed some distance behind by Sudan (7.4 per cent), Papua New Guinea (6.8 per cent) and Ethiopia (5.9 per cent). As Papua New Guinea only became a member of Stabex in Lomé II it has done well by comparison to countries which were members right from the beginning of Stabex in 1975.

Table 6.3 shows that by far the most important triggering products over the period 1975-87 were coffee (27.4 per cent) and groundnut products (22.0 per cent) followed, a long way behind, by cocoa (10.7 per cent). Groundnut products' share in Lomé I was 35.8

per cent but dropped to only 19.9 per cent in Lomé II. Coffee's share went up from 3.7 per cent to 36.8 per cent while that for cocoa increased from 0.4 per cent to 22.2 per cent. Iron ore was deleted from Lomé II, while the share for the important triggering product of cotton (11.1 per cent) in Lomé I was reduced by half and timber (10.3 per cent in Lomé I) did not feature at all in Lomé II.

Over the period of Lomé I and Lomé II, 271 separate transfers were made. Most of these (113) were claims for funds between 1 and 5 million Ecu each. There were 95 claims for funds between 100,000 and 1 million Ecu each. Thus nearly 77 per cent of all the claims were below 5 million Ecu each, showing the smallness in the vast majority of the requests for Stabex compensatory financing. There were only ten transfers which exceeded 20 million Ecu each and four which exceeded 40 million Ecu each.

The transfer funds were received usually between twelve and eighteen months after the end of the shortfall year, although advances could be requested. However, very few countries have made use of the advance facility. For example, under Lomé I only five countries (Dominica, Gambia, Mauritania, Senegal and Tonga) used it for a total of eight transfers. This amounted to only Ecu 33.8 million or 9 per cent of the total Stabex funds under Lomé I, and three of the five countries (Senegal, Mauritania and Gambia) accounted for 92 per cent of it.

Another important observation about the operation of Stabex is that there has not been much reimbursement of the transfers. Of the sixty-six ACP countries, forty-three are exempted from repayment because of their status as least developed, landlocked and island countries. The criteria for defining a country as least developed are less exacting than those used by the United Nations, as the number of least developed countries under Lomé III is greater than the number of UN least developed countries. The other twenty-three are formally required to repay the transfers received. However, some of them (e.g. Nigeria, Zimbabwe, Zambia and Zaire) do not draw from Stabex because their main exports are minerals which do not qualify for Stabex transfers. The other ACP countries eligible to repay reimbursed only Ecu 6.42 million over the 1975-80 period, either because the market for their Stabex-products had not recovered enough or because the Commission of the European Communities considered it politically imprudent to insist on repayment. Whatever the reason, the EEC has long ago abandoned the original idea of operating Stabex as a revolving fund. Since 1980, whatever reimbursements that have been made have only taken the form of deductions from new Stabex transfers. The main reimbursing countries in this much less painful repayment system are Cameroon, Ivory Coast, Fiji, Ghana and Madagascar. Thus in terms of the formal obligation to repay and the enforcement of it, the Stabex system is much more generous than the compensatory financing facility of the International Monetary Fund (IMF-CFF). The latter charges interest on its drawings and repayment is a regular and prominent feature of its operation.

7
Stabex: Impact on Export Instability and Economic Growth

Introduction

Stabex aims to mitigate the adverse effects of export instability on the economic growth of the ACP countries by stabilizing the income they earn from exporting certain products to the EEC. The scheme has been functioning since 1975 and the rules which govern its operation have been refined over time. The number of ACP countries has increased from forty-three in Lomé I to sixty-six in Lomé III. The number of eligible products has gone up from thirty-six to forty-eight. The funds set aside for it under the European Development Fund have also been increased from Ecu 375 million in Lomé I to Ecu 557 million in Lomé II and Ecu 925 million in Lomé III, thereby maintaining the value in real terms.

The continuation of Stabex in the Lomé agreements, the greater geographical and product spread of the scheme and the maintenance of its real funding level would suggest, *prima facie*, that Stabex has been successful in pursuing its aim of reducing the harmful effects of export instability on economic growth by reducing export instability. This chapter assesses the impact of Stabex on export instability in the ACP countries and on their economic growth.

Impact on Export Instability

The first detailed empirical study on the effectiveness of Stabex in reducing the export instability of the ACP countries was carried out by Herrmann (1982). A few years earlier, Treydte (1977) had published a piece which claimed that Stabex had contributed to the stabilization of export earnings of the ACP countries in the first two years of its existence. However, such a conclusion is not warranted from the data provided. While there were some useful general comments on the limitations of Stabex, no data were presented on the impact of Stabex payments on the export instability of the ACP countries.

The study by Herrmann (1982) examines the stabilization effect of Stabex on the earnings of the exports of nine ACP countries to the EEC during the period of Lomé I. The sample consisted of Senegal, the biggest recipient of Stabex funds during Lomé I, and other countries which were among the more important drawers of Stabex funds. The results are given in Table 7.1.

The relative deviation of the export revenue of the product concerned (without Stabex) from the "normal" export revenue was calculated for the year of payment in question. This may be called the "without Stabex relative dispersion". Then the relative dispersion of the Stabex-compensated export revenue of the product from the "normal" export revenue was calculated for the same year. This can be called the "with Stabex relative dispersion".

Where the two relative dispersions have the same sign, the use of Stabex transfers would have stabilized export earnings if the "without Stabex relative dispersion" is greater than the "with Stabex relative dispersion". Where the two relative dispersions have opposite signs, Stabex would have had a stabilizing effect if the absolute value of the "without Stabex relative dispersion" were greater than that of the "with Stabex relative dispersion".

The "normal" export revenue of the product was calculated in two ways. The first was as the average export revenue of the product in the four years preceding the year of payment (normal revenue I). This is, in fact, the method used by Stabex in establishing its reference level. The second was the logarithmic trend for a much longer period, 1971-78, but applied to all the products and for all the ACP countries studied (normal revenue II).

If, in line with Stabex practice, the average of the export earnings in the four years preceding the year of payment is used as the normal export revenue (normal revenue I), then Table 7.1 shows that there were six cases when the use of Stabex transfers had stabilized export earnings and six when they had destabilized them. If the stabilizing case due to the payment of a transfer in advance, that for groundnut oil and oil cake for Senegal were discounted, the weight of the evidence suggests that the operation of Stabex had destabilized, rather than stabilized, the export earnings of the ACP countries in the sample.

Table 7.1: Stabilization effect of Stabex on selected ACP countries, Lomé I 1975-79

ACP country	Relative deviation of export revenue in year of payment from "normal" export revenue					
	Normal revenue I			Normal revenue II		
(Year of application/ year of transfer/product)	Without Stabex	With Stabex	Effect[1]	Without Stabex	With Stabex	Effect[1]
Benin						
(1975/1976/cotton)	-56.0	2.5	S	-0.6	131.7	D
Cameroon						
(1975/1976/timber)	30.2	44.7	D	-5.0	5.6	D
Congo, P.R.						
(1975/1976/timber)	-33.0	50.8	D	-24.4	70.2	D
Ethiopia						
(1975/1976/coffee)	210.2	336.9	D	25.6	76.9	D
(1975/1976/raw skins and hides)	-57.6	158.4	D	32.6	708.7	D
Ghana						
(1975/1976/timber)	12.5	38.4	D	29.6	59.5	D
Ivory Coast						
(1975/1976/timber)	39.4	51.2	D	16.3	26.1	D
Niger						
(1976/1977/groundnut oil)	-83.3	-15.5	S	-34.0	234.1	D
(1977/1978/groundnut oil)	-79.3	16.3	S	-17.0	366.0	D
Senegal						
(1978/1979/groundnut oil and oil cake)	-42.2	-30.2	S	-47.0	-36.0	S
Tanzania						
(1976/1977/sisal)	-62.3	-37.5	S	-43.8	-6.9	S
(1977/1978/sisal)	-48.0	-7.5	S	-27.6	28.8	D

Source: Herrmann (1982), p. 9.

[1] S = stabilizing, D = destabilizing

The size of the destabilizing effects is, on average, much greater than that of the stabilizing effects (80 percentage points against 50 percentage points). The biggest destabilizing impact was experienced by Ethiopia. In the case of raw skins and hides the relative dispersion without the Stabex transfer was -57.6 per cent but increased to 158.4 per cent with the Stabex transfer, a change of 216 percentage points. In the case of coffee, the "without Stabex relative dispersion" was 210.2 per cent while the "with Stabex relative dispersion" was 336.9 per cent, an increase of 126.7 percentage points. The biggest stabilizing impact was in Niger, but the use of Stabex transfers provided decreases in the relative dispersion of only between 67.8 and 95.6 percentage points.

If the normal export revenue is calculated by fitting a logarithmic trend function for 1971-78 (normal revenue II), then the results show Stabex to have been even less successful in stabilizing export earnings. In only two of the twelve cases were the transfer of Stabex funds effective in reducing export instability (the advance payment to Senegal for shortfalls in the revenue from groundnut oil and oil cake and the payment to Tanzania for shortfalls in the revenue from sisal).

The markedly worse result in the stabilizing ability of Stabex when the normal export revenue is calculated by fitting a logarithmic trend line for 1971-78 suggests that the Stabex method of calculating the reference level (the benchmark for comparison) tends to underestimate the normal export revenue if there is a decrease in export earnings. When this underestimation is corrected, four of the stabilizing cases (Benin in 1976, Niger in 1977 and 1978, and Tanzania in 1978) turned out to be destabilizing.

The ineffectiveness of Stabex in stabilizing export earnings was also reported in a bigger and more comprehensive study by Herrmann (1983) over the period 1974-80. The sample consisted of nineteen ACP countries and included those which received the largest payments or the largest number of transfers. The results, given in Table 7.2, show that the operation of Stabex managed to stabilize the export earnings of only six of the nineteen countries, though in two of the six (Benin and Mauritania) the reduction in export instability was substantial. In one country (Gabon) Stabex made no difference but in the remaining twelve countries the receipt of Stabex transfers actually destabilized the situation.

The failure of Stabex as a stabilizing force was recognised by the governments of some of the recipient ACP countries. When asked for their views on Stabex, some of the heads of state of ten francophone countries admitted that Stabex did not fulfil any fundamental stabilization objectives (*Marchés Tropicaux*, 1985).

There are two reasons for the inability of Stabex to stabilize export earnings. First, the Stabex transfers are normally received twelve to eighteen months after the end of the shortfall year, and can therefore come when the export earnings of the product concerned are on the increase again. The net result of this is to increase rather than decrease export instability. In some cases the payments were made four years after the actual revenue loss and any stabilizing effect under such circumstances could only have been coincidental.

Table 7.2: Stabilization effect of Stabex on selected ACP countries, 1974-80

ACP country	Period	Instability index [1] (%) Export earnings without Stabex transfers	Export earnings with Stabex transfers	Percentage change in instability index (%)
Benin	1972-78	17.9	15.1	-15.6
Central African Republic	1973-79	13.5	13.3	-1.6
Congo	1971-77	26.1	25.8	-1.1
Ethiopia	1974-80	11.6	11.4	-1.6
Gambia	1974-80	23.3	25.8	+10.8
Gabon	1973-79	14.7	14.7	0.0
Ghana	1972-78	25.6	25.7	+0.2
Ivory Coast	1973-79	11.6	11.4	-1.5
Liberia	1974-80	4.6	4.7	+0.6
Mali	1974-80	14.6	14.9	+1.8
Mauritania	1974-80	15.4	11.9	-22.5
Niger	1971-79	16.9	18.3	+8.4
Senegal	1972-78	39.7	39.9	+0.5
Sudan	1974-80	19.0	19.5	+2.8
Swaziland	1973-79	10.1	10.2	+1.0
Tanzania	1974-80	16.9	17.3	+2.4
Uganda	1973-79	32.9	33.0	+0.3
Upper Volta	1974-80	16.3	17.0	+4.5
Western Samoa	1974-80	36.7	37.9	+3.3

Source: Hermann (1983), p. 20.

[1] The index is the one used by Cuddy and Della Valle (1978).

Stabex allows for the payment in advance of its transfers. The use of this facility required detailed monthly trade statistics to be available promptly, but is a price worth paying as it would have enhanced the stabilizing ability of Stabex. However, very few countries have made use of it. For example, under Lomé I only five ACP countries used it for the payment of eight transfers, which came to only Ecu 33.8 million or just 9 per cent of the total Stabex funding. The fact that so few countries have made use of advance payments suggests that stabilizing the export revenue of the triggering product may never have been the factor which sustains the EEC's support for Stabex nor the main reason for ACP countries applying for Stabex transfers.

The second reason for Stabex's failure as a stabilizing body is that it does not require that the funds be used to reduce fluctuations in the export revenue of the triggering sector. Thus in Lomé I the recipient ACP countries were allowed to decide how the Stabex funds were to be used (article 20). There was no reference or requirement that the funds had to be used in ways that were linked to the aims of the scheme. The only requirement was that the recipient ACP countries had to report within twelve months following the signature of the transfer agreement the ways in which the funds had been used.

In a study of thirty-nine transfers to ten ACP countries under Lomé I, totalling Ecu 206 million or 50 per cent of the total Stabex transfers and involving twelve products, Hewitt (1983) found that the absence of a formal requirement to use the funds in the sector which triggered the transfer was reflected in the ways in which the countries actually used the funds. Most of them did not use the funds to tackle the problems which brought about export instability in the triggering sectors.

Table 7.3 shows that supply factors (lower export volumes) were much more important than demand factors (lower export prices) in causing export earnings to be below the reference levels and, hence, for Stabex transfers to be requested and granted. The lower export volume was due largely to a long-term decline in production, caused in turn by the pursuit of negative pricing policy (Hewitt, 1983: 1019). Inadequate world demand and natural disasters, often presumed the major problems faced by primary producers, were not important reasons for the long-term decrease in output.

Table 7.4 shows that most of the Stabex funds were not used directly in reducing the gap between the reference level and the actual export revenue in the triggering sectors. Activities which would help the triggering sector include price support for the producers, the subsidization of extension services and inputs and the provision of project aid. In a large number of cases (copra and cloves in Comoros, coconut oil in Fiji, hides and skins in Sudan, cotton and sisal in Tanzania and cocoa and timber in Western Samoa) Stabex transfers were used entirely outside the triggering sectors. Only in one case, that of bananas in Western Samoa, were the funds employed totally in the triggering sector.

These findings led Hewitt to conclude that under Lomé I, while Stabex was product-linked in its triggering mechanism, it is "only weakly product-linked once the financial transfer is made" (1983:1010). The same conclusion may well be made of Lomé II. It appeared to be

Table 7.3: Causes of Stabex intervention

	Demand factors: Lower export prices	Supply factors: Lower export volume to EEC	Lower total export volume	Unspecified or unidentified
Cameroon				
Timber	X	X		
Cocoa paste		X		
Comoros				
Copra 1		X		
Copra 2			X	
Copra 3			X	
Copra 4			X	
Cloves 1	X		X	
Cloves 2	X		X	
Cloves 3	X		X	
Ylang-ylang			X	
Fiji				
Coconut oil 1	X	X		
Coconut oil 2	X	X		
Gambia				
Groundnuts 1978		X		
Groundnut oil 1979	X	X		
Groundnut cake 1979		X		
Groundnuts and groundnut oil 1980	X			
Mauritania				
Iron ore 1	X	X		
Iron ore 2	X	X		
Niger				
Groundnuts 1		X		
Groundnuts 2		X		
Groundnut oil 1		X		
Groundnut oil 2		X		
Oil cake		X		
Hides and skins				X
Senegal				
Groundnut oil 1978		X		
Oil cake 1978		X		
Groundnuts and groundnut oil 1980		X		
Oil cake 1980	X	X		
Sudan				
Groundnuts 1		X		
Groundnuts 2		X		
Groundnuts 3		X		
Hides and skins	X			
Sesame seeds		X		

(continued over)

Table 7.3 (continued)

	Demand factors: Lower export prices	Supply factors: Lower export volume to EEC	Lower total export volume	Unspecified or unidentified
Tanzania				
Cotton		X		
Sisal 1		X		
Sisal 2		X		
Sisal 3		X		
Western Samoa				
Cocoa 1 (1975)	X	X		
Cocoa 2 (1978)			X	
Copra	X		X	
Timber			X	
Bananas			X	

Source: Hewitt (1983), p. 1022.

Note: 'Lower' price and 'lower' volume are defined strictly in Stabex terms. Unit prices and export tonnage in the year for which the Stabex payment was made have to be lower than the average of the previous four years to qualify. Prices and tonnage which are simply lower than the previous year do not qualify, nor would such circumstances have triggered a Stabex transfer.

stricter over the use of Stabex funds as its first reference to it, in article 23, stated that the funds must be devoted to maintaining financial flows in the triggering sector. However, the second part of the article went on to negate this requirement by stating that for the purpose of diversification the funds could also be directed towards other appropriate sectors and used for economic and social development.

The same degree of ambiguity could be detected later on in Lomé II. In article 42 it permitted the recipient ACP countries to decide how the resources were to be used, provided that they complied with the objectives of Stabex. However, the exact nature of this compliance was never spelt out.

Article 42 also stated that when the ACP country's request for funds is assessed and before the transfer agreement is signed, the requesting country had to give the Commission of the European Communities some indication of the probable use of the funds. However, as with article 23, there was no requirement that the funds had to be used in the triggering sector. Consequently the need for the recipient ACP country to supply an *ex post* declaration on use could not ensure that the funds were in fact used for stabilizing export earnings in the triggering sector. Indeed, an ACP/EEC common declaration stated that the implementation of the Stabex transfer should not be made conditional on the indication of its probable use. This may reflect a tacit recognition that foreign aid funds are fungible and any insistence that they be spent on a specific project in a specific sector cannot be enforced effectively.

Table 7.4: Use of Stabex transfers by sector

	Inside the triggering sector				Outside	
	Projects	Price support	Revenue support	Other		
Cameroon						
Timber	*				***	
Cocoa paste			**		**	
Comoros						
Copra 1						?
Copra 2					****	
Copra 3					****	
Copra 4					****	
Cloves 1	*				***	
Cloves 2					****	
Cloves 3					****	
Ylang-ylang			**		**	
Fiji						
Coconut oil 1					****	
Coconut oil 2					****	
Gambia						
Groundnuts 1978			**		**	
Groundnut oil 1979			**		**	
Groundnut cake 1979			**		**	
Groundnuts and groundnut oil 1980			**		**	
Mauritania						
Iron ore 1				*	***	
Iron ore 2				*	***	
Niger						
Groundnuts 1		**			**	
Groundnuts 2		**			**	
Groundnut oil 1		**			**	
Groundnut oil 2		**			**	
Oil cake		*			**	
Hides and skins				*	***	
Senegal						
Groundnut oil 1978						
Oil cake 1978						
Groundnuts and groundnut oil 1980						?
Oil cake 1980						

(continued over)

Table 7.4 (continued)

	Inside the triggering sector				Outside	
	Projects	Price support	Revenue support	Other		
Sudan						
Groundnuts 1	**		**			
Groundnuts 2						?
Groundnuts 3						?
Hides and skins					****	
Sesame seeds						?
Tanzania						
Cotton					****	
Sisal 1	*				***	
Sisal 2					****	
Sisal 3					****	
Western Samoa						
Cocoa 1 (1975)					****	
Cocoa 2 (1978)	*				***	
Copra	*				***	
Timber					****	
Bananas	****					

Source: Hewitt (1983), p. 1023.

Note: **** Wholly; *** Mostly; ** Partly; * Only slightly; ? The evaluation in these cases was concerned with determining the proportion of the transfers used in the 'rural world' (put at 47%) and not specifically in the groundnut producing sector.

That Lomé II was not effective in ensuring that Stabex transfers were used mainly for reducing export instability in the triggering sector can be seen from the relatively much stronger position taken by Lomé III on the matter. While it still formerly allows recipient countries to argue the case for allocating the funds to sectors other than the one where the shortfall has occurred, it now has in place stricter administrative rules to ensure that the funds are spent in the ways indicated. Thus, if a recipient ACP country does not hand in a report on the use it has made of the funds within fourteen months of the signing of the agreement, the Commission of the European Communities can suspend the eligibility of the country for drawing on Stabex funds.

However, Lomé III still allows the ACP countries to make a case for using the Stabex funds in a non-triggering sector, and many of them do and for quite legitimate reasons. The most important of these is the long-term decline in the output in the triggering sector as a result of the secular decline in the commodity terms of trade. Under these conditions it would make more economic sense to use the Stabex transfers to diversify the economy rather than to prop up an economically non-viable activity.

Such a use of Stabex funds was given explicit recognition in a recent important joint publication of the Commission of the European Communities and the ACP countries, called *Stabex: User's Guide*, in the following way:

> An ACP state which receives a Stabex transfer is free to decide how the money is to be spent. Nevertheless, it must exercise its discretionary powers in conformity with the rules of the Convention, in particular that which states that transfers should be used to maintain financial flows in the sector in which the loss of earnings has occurred. Sometimes the situation in the sector concerned is such, however, that it would be pointless to shore up existing production structures, and the Convention therefore also provides that the money can be directed, for the purposes of diversification, to other sectors of the economy.

Given that it is possible to argue, under certain circumstances, for the use of Stabex funds for diversification purposes, and given official recognition of this, it is not surprising that many recipient ACP countries do not use the funds in the triggering sectors. This practice could explain why Stabex has not been effective in stabilizing the export revenue of the sector which triggered the transfer.

Impact on Economic Growth

The analysis so far shows that Stabex has not been able to reduce export instability in the triggering sector. The reasons for this failure are the lag in the receipt of the transfers and the widespread practice of not using the funds in the triggering sector.

However, the finding that Stabex has not been effective in stabilizing export earnings does not automatically mean that it has not contributed to the economic growth of the recipient ACP countries. It might not have been able to promote economic growth by mitigating the harmful effects of export instability, but it could have contributed to growth by other more effective ways. Whether it has actually done so depends importantly on the size of the Stabex transfers in relation to the ACP countries' developmental need and on the ways in which the transfers have been used.

It has been shown that very little of the Stabex transfers have been reimbursed because of the large number of countries exempted and because those countries which are formally obliged to repay have never been seriously requested to do so. It has also been pointed out that in reality Stabex transfers are untied and without the need for repayment the transfers are in fact untied budgetary support, the most generous form of foreign aid. The question of the impact of Stabex on economic growth then becomes one of the impact of untied budgetary support on economic growth. What this impact is depends on the level of this aid and the ways in which the recipient countries have used it.

The operation of Stabex is small compared to that for the IMF-CFF. Over the period which covered Lomé I and Lomé II, 1975-84, an amount equal to US$12 billion was drawn from the IMF-CFF. By comparison the amount of Stabex transfers came to only US$1.2 billion. Over the same period, while the IMF-CFF drawings accounted for 25 per cent of all the credit extended by the International Monetary Fund, Stabex transfers made up only 10 per cent of the European Development Fund of the EEC.

However, the comparative smallness of Stabex transfers does not mean that the amounts are not important in relation to the developmental needs of the recipient ACP countries. First, a large number of them are very small economies, some of them being really mini-states. Second, many of them are least developed countries, with very low per capita incomes. Under Lomé III, forty-three of the sixty-six ACP countries have this status. Third, many of the ACP countries have large budget deficits where any extra revenue would be welcome. Table 7.5 shows that twenty-nine of the thirty-two recipient ACP countries for which data were available had central government budget deficits during Lomé I. Under Lomé II, again twenty-nine of the thirty-two countries had budget deficits. Fourth, many of the ACP countries have severe balance-of-payments problems. Table 7.5 shows that twenty-three of the thirty-eight countries for which data were available had balance-of-payments deficits during Lomé I. The situation during Lomé II was worse as thirty-two of the forty-three countries for which data were available experienced balance-of-payments deficits. As Stabex transfers are made largely in French Francs, Deutschmarks and Sterling and the little repayment that goes on can be made in local currencies, the availability of any amount of international currencies would be invaluable.

The combination of their relative smallness, low level of income, central government budget deficit and balance-of-payments deficit has

Table 7.5: Stabex transfers, central government budget and balance-of-payments of selected ACP countries, Lomé I and II

ACP country	Lomé I				Lomé II			
	Central government budget (CGB) (US$m)	Stabex transfers/ CGB (%)	Balance of payments (BP) (US$m)	Stabex transfers/ BP (%)	Central government budget (CGB) (US$m)	Stabex transfers/ CGB (%)	Balance of payments (BP) (US$m)	Stabex transfers/ BP (%)
Belize	na	na	na	na	na	na	-5	0
Benin	24	66	-50	53	na	na	-120	4
Burkina Faso	-12	78	-49	19	-39	3	94	1
Burundi	8	24	na	na	-58	25	na	na
Cameroon	17	31	-23	23	-60	52	22	141
Cape Verde	na	na	na	na	na	na	na	na
Central African Republic	na	na	24	42	na	na	-58	9
Chad	-22	43	-60	16	na	na	13	54
Comoros	na	na	na	na	-50	14	0	0
Congo	na	na	-57	17	-384	0	-87	0
Djibouti	na	na	na	na	na	na	na	na
Dominica	-6	62	7	53	na	na	-13	29
Ethiopia	-705	3	-151	12	-345	3	-184	6
Fiji	-105	3	27	10	-210	1	-5	63
Gabon	-874	1	-90	10	261	0	309	0
Gambia	-56	17	-25	39	-62	31	-101	19
Ghana	-4280	0.2	-32	21	5957	2	-454	20
Grenada	-12	0	3	0	2	208	-9	46
Guinea-Bissau	na	na	na	na	na	na	na	na
Ivory Coast	-739	3	-157	12	-992	10	-2125	5
Jamaica	-1977	0	-701	0	-2225	0.2	-711	0.6
Kenya	-913	0	162	0	-1251	4	-684	7
Kiribati	na	na	na	na	na	na	na	na
Lesotho	-29	0	-4	0	-59	2	87	2
Liberia	-234	4	-94	10	-479	0	-503	0
Madagascar	na	na	-183	4	na	na	-942	1
Malawi	-324	0	-65	0	-545	1	-205	3
Mali	-56	22	-112	11	-404	3	-108	10
Mauritania	-152	31	-78	61	na	na	-159	0
Niger	-156	19	53	55	-77	0	-100	0
Papua New Guinea	-	-	-	-	-470	11	-27	197
Rwanda	-63	1	142	1	-20	49	-31	32
Sao Tome	na	na	26	0	na	na	-48	17
Senegal	-88	95	-108	78	-383	25	-310	31
Sierra Leone	-342	2	-133	4	-661	2	-445	3

(continued over)

Table 7.5 (continued)

ACP country	Lomé I				Lomé II			
	Central government budget (CGB) (US$m)	Stabex transfers/ CGB (%)	Balance of payments (BP) (US$m)	Stabex transfers/ BP (%)	Central government budget (CGB) (US$m)	Stabex transfers/ CGB (%)	Balance of payments (BP) (US$m)	Stabex transfers/ BP (%)
Solomon Islands	-3	93	33	8	-42	11	40	11
Somalia	-200	1	19	13	na	na	-119	3
Sudan	-1607	3	-942	6	-590	7	-1790	2
St Lucia	-3	0	7	0	-14	12	-5	34
St Vincent	na	0	4	0	-5	19	-1	96
Swaziland	-43	40	96	18	-76	11	28	31
Tanzania	-1326	2	318	8	-2104	1	-1017	2
Togo	-510	1	-18	26	-116	26	167	18
Tonga	na	na	7	22	na	na	11	38
Tuvalu	na	na	na	na	na	na	-2	7
Uganda	-932	3	-113	23	-482	0	-441	0
Vanuatu	na	na	na	na	na	na	-4	234
Western Samoa	na	na	-9	41	1	681	3	227

Note: In some cases data on the central government budget and the balance-of-payments were not available for the entire duration of Lomé I (1975-79) and Lomé II (1980-84). In such cases (Benin, Comoros, Congo, Ethiopia, Gabon, Grenada, Ivory Coast, Lesotho, Niger, Rwanda, Western Samoa, Senegal, Sudan and Togo), the shares of Stabex in the central government budget and the balance-of-payments were calculated on a per annual basis.

meant that for many recipient ACP countries the receipt of Stabex transfers has reduced their budget and balance-of-payments deficits quite substantially. This is brought out clearly in Table 7.5. For example, during Lomé I, the receipt of Stabex transfers was equal to over 90 per cent of the central government deficits in the Solomon Islands and Senegal. In Burkina Faso and Dominica the respective figures were 78 per cent and 62 per cent. In the case of balance-of-payments deficits, Stabex transfers made up 78 per cent, 61 per cent and 53 per cent of the deficit in Senegal, Mauritania and Benin respectively. The share was over 20 per cent for Cameroon, Gambia, Ghana, Western Samoa, Togo and Uganda. Stabex transfers also played a significant role in financing budget and balance-of-payments deficits in many ACP countries during Lomé II.

Whether Stabex transfers, which are significant in relation to the developmental needs of the recipient ACP countries, will actually promote their economic growth will depend on the use these countries make of the transfers. If the funds were used for building mansions for ministers of the state, then the developmental impact of Stabex will be negligible. If, on the other hand, they were used for development expenditure in properly formulated and implemented agricultural projects, then the developmental impact would be more noticeable.

The study by Hewitt (1983) provides some information on the use of Stabex transfers in ten ACP countries during Lomé I. It is clear from the study that most of the transfers were used on activities outside the triggering sectors. It is also clear that the funds were spent outside the triggering sectors in different ways by different countries. In some they were allocated to the development budget with the spending proposals being placed before parliament for approval. In others they were used for recurrent government expenditure, with the transfers being channelled through extra-budgetary accounts. The nature of the development expenditures also varied. Some countries used the funds for agricultural diversification programmes while others spent them on infrastructural projects. The programmes of current public consumption were also varied, and could include, although not in the ten ACP countries studied, the purchase of Mercedes cars and the conduct of a civil war.

It can be argued that, *ceteris paribus*, those countries which use their Stabex transfers as development expenditures are more likely to grow faster than those which use them as consumption expenditure. However, using the transfers as development expenditures is not a guarantee that economic growth will be accelerated as it depends on the efficiency with which the expenditure programmes are formulated and implemented.

Therein lies one of the problems in assessing the impact of Stabex transfers on economic growth. Very detailed information is required on the development expenditure, as well as on the recurrent expenditure, as the two often complement each other. The study by Hewitt does not produce such information and Hewitt himself does not come to any conclusion about the impact of Stabex on economic growth.

Another problem is that the impact captured may only be a partial one. The literature on foreign aid shows that even when aid is given for development expenditure on a specific project, it can still increase consumption expenditure elsewhere in the economy. The government of the recipient country can simply use the domestic resources which have been set aside for the development project, if aid had not been forthcoming, for consumption purposes elsewhere if aid was in fact given. The availability of aid (Stabex) funds could then have allowed the recipient country to be less careful about its overall expenditure programme and the net effect on its economic performance could be negligible.

Part III
Need for a New Facility

8
UNCTAD's Supplementary Scheme

Introduction

The review of the literature on the causes of export instability and the effect of this instability on economic growth produces three important conclusions. First, at the commodity and country level, supply instability is more important in explaining earnings instability than price instability. Second, policies and mechanisms are needed to reduce the instability of commodities supplied at the individual commodity and country level. Third, export instability slows down economic growth through a number of avenues, of which only one is related to the balance-of-payments.

The examination of the provisions and the operation of the IMF-CFF also produces three important conclusions. First, it has not been able to reduce the instability of export earnings because a number of its provisions act against that. Second, it sets out to stabilize export earnings rather than deal with the factors which produce the export instability. By choosing to deal with the effects rather than the causes of supply instability, it cannot prevent instability from recurring. Third, by linking the provision of compensatory finance to a balance-of-payments need, it can effectively deal with only one of the channels through which export instability can harm economic growth. The analysis of the operation of Stabex shows that it also has not been able to reduce export fluctuations. While Stabex is designed as a commodity-specific compensatory financing scheme, it has not required that the transfer be used for compensating purposes in the commodity sector which triggered the transfer in the first place. The recipient countries have responded accordingly by using the funds largely in the non-triggering sectors. In reality, Stabex operates as a vehicle for channelling European foreign aid. A large percentage of the ACP recipients of Stabex funds are not required to repay the loans because of their status as least developed, landlocked and island states. As the qualifying criteria for this status have been kept much less demanding than those set by the United Nations, the granting of aid has obviously been planned as an important feature of the scheme. This is more or less confirmed by the fact that very few of the recipients which are expected to repay the transfers have actually done so and have been under no real pressure from Stabex to do so. Another criticism of Stabex is that its coverage is limited only to the ACP countries and it excludes a number of commodities which feature prominently in the exports of some ACP countries.

These criticisms of the IMF-CFF and Stabex and the apparent unwillingness of the International Monetary Fund and the European Community to change the fundamental nature of their schemes have led some to argue for the establishment of a new facility which is better able to deal with the causes of export instability. In particular, UNCTAD has been prompted to argue very strongly for the establishment of a new scheme to supplement the IMF-CFF.

History

At its first session in 1964, UNCTAD requested the World Bank to prepare a study on an additional compensatory financing facility to supplement the IMF-CFF. This study was duly completed in late 1965 and recommended a scheme to provide additional funds for compensating export shortfalls that was based on the general disruptive effects of shortfalls on development planning, and not just on a balance-of-payments need (World Bank, 1965). It recognized that some of the problems caused by unexpected shortfalls could not be dealt with by the granting of short-term balance-of-payments support only. An Intergovernmental Group on Supplementary Financing was subsequently set up in September 1966 by the Trade and Development Board of UNCTAD to examine the World Bank scheme. This reported in 1969 that the proposed scheme was workable, but recommended that the new facility be administered within the World Bank in consultation with the IMF.

The Trade and Development Board of UNCTAD accepted these conclusions and invited the World Bank to work out the details of the scheme. However, in August 1970, the World Bank informed UNCTAD that it had decided to defer consideration of the scheme as there was very little support among potential donors for contributing the extra funds required to operate the scheme.

Although the matter was raised by UNCTAD again, including at its third session in May 1972, the idea went no further until September 1975, when the United States' government proposed a new facility to stabilize export earnings at the Seventh Special Session of the General Assembly of the United Nations (United Nations, 1975). It saw economic security as fundamental for international economic development and a new approach to reduce the drastic fluctuations in the export earnings of developing countries was considered to be an important feature of any programme to produce this security.

This concern for export stability arose from the acknowledgement that the development programmes of many developing countries depend heavily on earnings from the export of primary commodities and that such earnings fluctuate a great deal. For countries with low reserves and a poor international credit rating, export shortfalls usually lead to reductions in the import of intermediate and capital goods crucial to their investment programmes.

Thus, the United States' government saw that the unpredictability of export earnings could make a mockery of development planning. It therefore proposed the establishment, within the International Monetary Fund, of a new development security facility to stabilize overall export earnings.

It was careful to stress that the proposal was not one to stabilize prices, as for many commodities price stabilization could only be achieved by restricting very severely either their production or export by operating expensive buffer stocks, or by maintaining prices at levels which encouraged the introduction of substitutes.

The proposal was to introduce a scheme to stabilize export earnings which would be more comprehensive than the existing IMF-CFF and which would replace it. Thus, the scheme would cover export earnings not only from primary commodities but also from manufactured goods. It would provide bigger loans of up to $2.5 billion or more a year, with a potential total in outstanding loans of $10 billion. The poorest countries would be allowed to convert their loans into grants under certain conditions. Also, it would be operated differently to the IMF-CFF as the drawings could be made "part automatically, part subject to balance-of-payments conditions and part reserved for cases of particularly violent swings in commodity earnings" (United Nations, 1975: paragraph 71:7). The IMF-CFF is to be called upon, it will be recalled, only when there is a balance-of-payments need.

The United States' government finished off its presentation by saying that its proposal would provide unprecedented protection against the disruptions caused by unexpected reductions in export earnings. The funds available from the new scheme would reinforce the traditional types of assistance from the United States, for without the stabilization of export earnings the benefits of its concessional aid to developing countries would be reduced. It also saw the proposal as benefiting the industrial countries, as the resulting healthier economies of the developing countries would provide the former with a steadier export market.

The position taken by the government of the United States was surprising as it had never been known to have been particularly supportive of the argument that export instability was detrimental to economic growth. The speed at which it said it would push the whole scheme through was also surprising as it announced that it would present its detailed proposals to the board of directors of the IMF by the end of the month (September 1975).

However, nothing came of the initiative and the United States reverted to its traditional and strongly held position that it is sceptical of the argument that instability is harmful to growth and that, if it is to support compensatory financing, this has to be based on balance-of-payments considerations.

The establishment of Stabex in 1975 by the European Community encouraged UNCTAD to continue its quest, as did the proposals by the Swedish and the West German governments in 1977 and 1978 respectively to set up an additional compensatory financing scheme. The Swedish scheme proposed compensating shortfalls in the total export earnings from all primary commodities, except fuels, gold and precious stones, for non-oil exporting countries. The shortfalls were to be calculated from a medium-term trend value of the export earnings in real terms and the loans to be given without any conditionality except that the applicant must first try to obtain compensation from the IMF-CFF. The repayments were to be based on the extent to which export earnings exceeded the trend values. For the least developed countries the loans were to be written off after five years and they were entitled to concessions on the interest rates. A quarter of the funds for the scheme were to come from direct capital contributions from the developed countries and the rest from borrowing on the international capital markets.

The Swedish proposal was followed a year later by a West German one to compensate shortfalls in the total export earnings from twenty-five commodities. The shortfalls were to be estimated using the IMF-CFF formula and full compensations were to be given for shortfalls above the threshold level. The loans were to be repaid within eight to ten years at interest rates significantly below the market rates and with special treatment for the least developed countries. A fund of $5 billion was to be raised for operating the scheme, part of which was to come from direct government contributions and part from international borrowing against government guarantees.

At UNCTAD V in May 1979, the Secretary-General of UNCTAD was asked to prepare a detailed study on the operation of a complementary facility to compensate shortfalls in the export earnings of individual commodities. Over the period 1980-83 the UNCTAD Secretariat estimated the shortfalls in the export earnings of a list of commodities (which included eighteen of the commodities in the Integrated Programme for Commodities and five others), carried out a feasibility study on the complementary facility (UNCTAD, 1981) and examined various proposals for setting it up.

The work carried out by the UNCTAD Secretariat and the reports emanating from it did not lead to a formal UNCTAD proposal for an additional compensatory facility. However, it did keep the debate alive on whether or not there should be such a facility and on the forms it could take and the costs incurred should one be established. The members of the UNCTAD Secretariat responsible for producing the studies were keen to set up an additional compensatory facility as they believed that the IMF-CFF, Stabex and the World Bank's structural adjustment schemes were not effective in dealing with the causes of export instability. They would have been joined by the governments of many developing countries which either were genuine in their belief that existing programmes could not provide long-term solutions to the problems caused by export instability or saw the campaign for an additional compensatory financing scheme as another opportunity to obtain more economic assistance from developed countries.

It was therefore not surprising that at UNCTAD VI in July 1983, the Secretary-General of UNCTAD was asked to convene an Expert Group on the compensatory financing of shortfalls in export earnings, with the group to complete its work by the end of September 1984. The governments of member countries were also asked to submit their views by the end of 1983, so that these could be considered by the Expert Group in the preparation of its report.

The report of the Expert Group was published in early 1985 (UNCTAD, 1985) in which it presented a prototype of a new facility which linked the uses of commodity-specific compensatory finance to the needs of supply adjustment programmes. The next section will present the views of those member-countries of UNCTAD which responded to the call for submissions to the Expert Group, to be followed by one which sets out the details of the Expert Group's prototype for a new compensatory financing facility.

Views of Governments on Compensatory Financing

Sixteen member countries of UNCTAD responded to the request for views on the need for an additional compensatory financing scheme. Ten of these were developed countries: Australia, Canada, Finland, France, West Germany, Italy, Norway, Sweden, Switzerland and the USA. Five were developing countries: one from Asia (Burma), three from Africa (Madagascar, Morocco and Senegal) and one from the Indian Ocean (Mauritius). The oil-rich country of Saudi Arabia also sent in its views. There was also a response from the European Economic Community.

The response was a poor one, both in the number of respondents and in the quality of the submissions. This was especially the case with the developing countries. The submissions from Madagascar and Mauritius were very short and said nothing substantial. The Burmese response was even shorter but it did say that it was not keen on the idea of a new compensatory financing facility and preferred an increase in the quota provided by the IMF-CFF as a response to the problem. The submission from Saudi Arabia simply said that it had no observations or proposals to make. The returns from Morocco and Senegal were more substantial. Morocco took a balanced position, arguing for an improved IMF-CFF and the need for a number of important questions to be answered before a new facility is established. Senegal, an important recipient of Stabex transfers, argued very strongly for a new facility as it believed that the IMF-CFF and Stabex were not very effective. However, it did not back up its claims with detailed arguments.

This was the sum total of the contributions from the developing world. Developing countries such as Malaysia, Ivory Coast, Ghana and Papua New Guinea, which possess features that, *prima facie*, would make them susceptible to the adverse effects of export instability, did not make any submissions. The relative lack of response from developing countries could be due to many factors. One is the belief that it is a lost cause. Another is that UNCTAD is already doing a good job for them in pushing for a new compensatory financing facility. Yet another reason could be the feeling that the case is not strong: their needs are already catered for quite adequately by the IMF-CFF and Stabex and whatever needs are not could be tackled domestically.

The responses from the developed countries are far more substantial and came from countries which had previously made proposals and suggestions concerning the need for a commodity-related compensatory financing facility. The responses can be divided into three categories: three which are against the idea, one which is keen and six which are open-minded.

The case against the establishment of an additional compensatory financing scheme was led by the USA. In a strongly-worded submission, it argued that there was no case for a study to establish whether or not there is a need for a new facility as it believed that the IMF-CFF was playing the compensatory role adequately. It saw balance-of-payments problems as being caused, more often than not, by inappropriate domestic policies and the establishment of a new and more liberal complementary scheme would only delay necessary structural change in developing countries. New proposals for additional compensatory schemes were seen by the American submission as only proposals for more foreign aid.

The Australian submission was also not enthusiastic. It emphasized that the need was to deal with the causes and not the effects of export instability. Export diversification, industrial restructuring and, somewhat surprisingly, price stabilization through the use of international commodity agreements were seen as more appropriate instruments. It saw a need for compensatory financing but felt that the IMF-CFF was doing a good supplementary job. The Italian government was not keen as it believed that the establishment of a new compensatory financing facility would discourage diversification and rationalization. It saw as a more pressing requirement the extension of Stabex to all the least less developed countries.

The only country which showed any enthusiasm at all for setting up an additional facility was France. The submission reveals a very strong support for compensatory financing schemes in general. It argues for establishing a separate facility for the least less developed countries along Stabex lines, on the grounds that these suffer serious deterioration in their terms of trade.

Six countries (Canada, Finland, West Germany, Norway, Sweden and Switzerland) made what can be described as sensible and open-minded submissions. Most made the point that the adverse effects of export instability on economic growth had to be established first, to be followed by an analysis which shows that the IMF-CFF and Stabex had not help to mitigate the adverse effects. Only after then could the case for an additional facility be made. Most of the submissions then argued for a net approach to earnings from primary commodities and some believed that it should be limited to the least less developed countries. The most substantial of these responses, and of all the sixteen responses, came from Canada, which gave a well researched, presented and written submission, complete with a comprehensive bibliography on the existence, causes and effects of export earnings instability.

In its submission, the European Economic Community pointed out that it has always been concerned with the problems created by export instability, and was exploring ways of extending the operation of Stabex to cover developing countries which are not members of the Lomé Convention. It was therefore prepared to examine any proposal for an additional compensatory financing facility with an open mind.

A summary of the views of the European Economic Community and of the sixteen countries is given in Table 8.1. The table also contains the main features of the schemes proposed by the USA, Sweden and West Germany in 1975, 1977 and 1978 respectively.

UNCTAD's Additional Compensatory Facility

The Expert Group consisted of nineteen members from nineteen countries, ten of which were developed (USA, Canada, West Germany, France, Australia, Sweden, Japan, USSR, Poland and Hungary) and nine developing (India, Indonesia, China, Algeria, Kenya, Ghana, Brazil, Venezuela and Trinidad and Tobago).

Its composition reflected the need for an acceptable mixture of developed and developing countries, of Asian, African and Central and South American developing countries, and of market and socialist economies. Among the developing countries were those which, *prima facie*, had no problems associated with export instability but had clearly been included because of their influence in world affairs. The developed non-socialist countries represented were largely those which had shown a great deal of interest in the debate either because they saw a need for compensatory finance in general or because they saw such schemes as another unjustified attempt to obtain more foreign aid.

The occupational distribution of the members was also interesting. Among the ten representatives from the developed countries, six worked in universities or research institutes and four of these had published extensively in the area of export instability. Of the

Table 8.1: Main characteristics of proposals and suggestions made by governments and the UNCTAD Secretariat in connection with additional commodity-related compensatory financing facilities

Proposer and date	Country coverage for access to drawings	Commodity coverage	Compensation criterion	Capital structure	Terms and concessionality	Relations to IMF-CFF	Conditions
United States 1975	Developing countries	15 commodities (including IPC 10 core)		IMF Trust Fund financed in part out of proceeds of IMF gold sales and from medium-term borrowing	For poorer countries: 2-3 per cent interest rates and 10-12 years repayment periods. Other developing countries: interest rate to cover cost of financing and repayment period of 5-8 years	Must have fully utilized the initial 25 per cent of quota available under IMF-CFF	Existence of a balance-of-payments problem. Policy conditions, including commodity supply conditions
Sweden 1977 (revised 1983)	Developing countries	All primary commodities (except fuels),	Medium-term trend value of commodity	A scheme based on 25 per cent capital	In principle, repayment based on	Must first make use of all means to obtain	

(continued over)

Table 8.1 (continued)

Proposer and date	Country coverage for access to drawings	Commodity coverage	Compensation criterion	Capital structure	Terms and concessionality	Relations to IMF-CFF	Conditions
Sweden (continued)		i.e. SITC 0-2 4 and 68	export earnings in real terms	contributions from governments and borrowing on international capital markets	overage. For poorest countries compensation loans outstanding after 5 years to be written off. Subsidization of 5 per cent interest	compensation from IMF-CFF	
Federal Republic of Germany 1978 (revised 1984)	Developing countries	25 selected commodities	Based on IMF-CFF formula. Full compensation for shortfalls above threshold level	$5 billion over 10 years. Government contributions and funds raised in capital market with government	Loans running 8 to 10 years at interest significantly below market rates. Special treatment for the poorest	Account to be taken of payments under IMF-CFF	Some international monitoring (or conditionality)

(continued over)

Table 8.1 (continued)

Proposer and date	Country coverage for access to drawings	Commodity coverage	Compensation criterion	Capital structure	Terms and concessionality	Relations to IMF-CFF	Conditions
Federal Rep. of Germany (continued)				guarantees as backing	developing countries		
UNCTAD Secretariat 1981	Developing countries	All primary commodities (except fuels, gold, diamonds and precious stones) or some selective list like the IPC 18 commodities	Based on medium-term trend value in real terms	Based on 10 per cent government paid-in capital and borrowing on private capital markets, backed by callable capital subscribed by governments	Based on average and fixed maximum repayment period of 10 years. Highly concessional terms for least developed countries. For other countries rates approaching average interest cost of borrowing	Account to be taken of drawing under IMF-CFF to avoid double compensation	Mutual agreement between facility and client countries on use of credits relating to commodity problems and root causes of commodity supply instability

(continued over)

Table 8.1 (continued)

Proposer and date	Country coverage for access to drawings	Commodity coverage	Compensation criterion	Capital structure	Terms and concessionality	Relations to IMF-CFF	Conditions
Finland 1983	Least developed countries and countries most dependent on commodity export earnings	Commodity sector	Based on overall losses in earnings in commodity sector, in nominal terms, with fluctuation and dependence thresholds		No transfer of real resources	Compensation must be additional, with due account taken of existing facilities	Due consideration paid to need for structural adjustment policies and appropriate production planning in developing countries
Sweden 1983	Poor and very commodity-dependent countries				No transfer of real resources, more favourable terms for least developed countries		Market orientation, including necessary structural adjustments

(continued over)

Table 8.1 (continued)

Proposer and date	Country coverage for access to drawings	Commodity coverage	Compensation criterion	Capital structure	Terms and concessionality	Relations to IMF-CFF	Conditions
Norway 1983	Low-income countries with heavy dependence on commodity exports	All IPC at a minimum		Identify all sources (government contributions, borrowing on capital market, auto-financing, etc.)	Some concessionality	Full use of existing schemes first	
Senegal 1983	Developing countries	IPC + food products	Compensation for recorded production losses and coverage of costs of durable solutions to eliminating causes of these losses	By developed countries plus levy on verified overages from commodities covered in countries benefiting from system	Repayments linked to level of surplus, within 10 years maximum period		Financing arrangements should be such as to permit durable solutions to be found to eliminating the root causes of production shortfalls

(continued over)

Table 8.1 (continued)

Proposer and date	Country coverage for access to drawings	Commodity coverage	Compensation criterion	Capital structure	Terms and concessionality	Relations to IMF-CFF	Conditions
Federal Republic of Germany 1984	Developing countries obtaining at least half of their total earnings from commodities	All non-energy commodities	Aggregate decline in commodity exports to all countries, due to events outside control of country; use of IMF-CFF formula, or average of past data; possibility longer reference period: 10% trigger threshold (2.5% for LDCs). Compensation,	Revolving fund open to all countries; 1/3 government contributions, 2/3 from capital market, with fixed ceiling; contribution scale based on formula similar to the UN scale; contributions split into several instalments	Loans of 8-10 years maturity, repayments also if exports above trend (10% above mean value). Interest rate below market rate (lower for LDCs). Some remission of debts for poorest countries	Avoid double compensation	Repayment obligations should offer exporting countries an additional incentive to eliminate the cause of their loss of export earnings themselves, as far as it is in their power to do so

(continued over)

Table 8.1 (continued)

Proposer and date	Country coverage for access to drawings	Commodity coverage	Compensation criterion	Capital structure	Terms and concessionality	Relations to IMF-CFF	Conditions
Federal Republic of Germany (continued)			100% of shortfall for LDCs, 60-80% for others, depending on ceiling for funds				
France 1984	Priority to least developed countries		Favours the establishment of a 'distinct' facility along the lines of STABEX				
Switzerland 1984	In order of priority: least developed countries, low-income developing countries and other	All primary commodities except fuels, gold and precious stones (SITC 0, 1, 2, 4 and 68)	A formula which has proven itself, e.g. the calculation method used in the framework of the IMF-	Loans, based on government contributions and guarantees and borrowing on capital markets	More favourable terms to LDCs; repayments when overages in earnings occur, with fixed ultimate	Additional: avoid double compensation	Loans should encourage a producing country to adjust its production structure, mainly by its own means, in order

(continued over)

Table 8.1 (continued)

Proposer and date	Country coverage for access to drawings	Commodity coverage	Compensation criterion	Capital structure	Terms and concessionality	Relations to IMF-CFF	Conditions
Switzerland (continued)	developing countries strongly dependent on export of commodities		CFF, adapted to the commodity sector; partial compensation for shortfalls in commodity-related export earnings; consider using real values		time limit		to avoid the situation deteriorating to the point where a large-scale international action becomes necessary; loans should also support structural adjustment programmes which are in process, but the realization of which is hampered by shortfalls; possible use of

(continued over)

Table 8.1 (continued)

Proposer and date	Country coverage for access to drawings	Commodity coverage	Compensation criterion	Capital structure	Terms and concessionality	Relations to IMF-CFF	Conditions
Switzerland (continued)							national stabilization funds to carry out and co-ordinate policies
Australia 1984	Least developed and other low-income countries heavily dependent on export earnings from commodities	Commodities exported by these countries representing a crucial source of income (except oil and precious stones)		Contribution from as many countries as possible (industrialized plus oil exporters), representing finance additional to current development assistance	Overall ceiling per country for drawings from all facilities	Complementary to existing facilities; avoid double compensation	Necessary adjustment processes undertaken

Source: UNCTAD (1985), Annex VIII, pp. 1-3.

other four members, three worked in business and one in government and, as far as can be judged, they had not carried out any direct work on the issues concerned.

Of the nine members from the developing countries, six worked in government, two in universities and one in business. Very few of these could be said to have carried out research on issues related to export instability, but the majority of them would have had to deal with these issues in their work.

The Expert Group met three times in 1984 and worked very closely with the Commodities Division of the UNCTAD Secretariat to produce the report by early 1985. The actual writing of the report was carried out by the UNCTAD Secretariat with help from a drafting group of the Expert Group.

The Expert Group recommended that an additional compensatory facility be set up. It based this on the argument that the IMF-CFF and Stabex do not and cannot deal with the causes of export instability and the entire range of the harmful effects of export instability on economic growth. It is not based on the criticism that the two facilities have not been able to stabilize export earnings. The stabilizing capacity of the IMF-CFF can, in fact, be improved by introducing symmetry in the requirements for drawings and repaying so that countries repay when there is an export surplus and a favourable balance-of-payments position. It may also be improved by making even shorter the time-lag between the occurrence of a shortfall and the receipt of the funds drawn. The adoption of a better method for estimating the trend used for working out the shortfall will also help. These are all changes that can be carried out within the existing IMF-CFF system.

The Expert Group's scheme, which can be called the UNCTAD facility for short, has three major features. First, the loans are to be used to deal with the causes of export instability. As these causes are seen to originate mainly from the supply side at the commodity and country level, the loans are to be used to deal with the causes, rather than the effects, of supply instability. This would bring about a reduction in supply and earnings instability on a more permanent basis. Thus the loans cannot be used merely to maintain the stability of incomes from specific commodities. Second, the loans are to be based on shortfalls in export earnings calculated on a gross (i.e. commodity by commodity) rather than on a net (i.e. aggregated) basis, and are to be given even when there is not a balance-of-payments need. Third, the scheme is to be run along self-financing commercial lines, except for the least developed countries where a subsidized interest rate will be charged.

The three major features of the UNCTAD facility make it a fundamentally different operation to the IMF-CFF. By not tying its use to balance-of-payments needs, it attempts to deal with the entire range of economic ills emanating from export instability. Technically all of the countries represented in Figure 5.1 of this study are eligible. By adopting a gross, as opposed to a net, approach to estimating shortfalls from exports of primary commodities, it is also a more liberal scheme than the IMF-CFF. By tackling the causes of supply uncertainty, it could prevent export instability from recurring. By making the operation a basically self-financing one, it is not set up as another organization for transferring foreign aid.

Three broad categories of programmes are suggested for eliminating the causes of supply instability. The first consists of measures which reduce the impact of inclement weather on primary production. For example, the use of the compensatory finance for setting up crop rehabilitation and relocation programmes and for irrigation and water control schemes can help to reduce the adverse impact of droughts and heavy rains on production.

The second consists of measures to reduce instability in the supply and cost of important inputs such as seeds, fertilizers and pesticides. Thus the facility can provide the funds to a member country to purchase, stock and then distribute these inputs to ensure their steady supply.

The third consists of national price and income stabilization measures to reduce the risks and uncertainties faced by primary producers. Thus compensating finance can be used to establish marketing boards in order to stabilize income.

The Expert Group decided against setting up a new institution to operate the scheme. The establishment costs would be prohibitive and a new institution, without an established credit rating, would have to maintain a higher paid-in capital ratio and to pay less favourable rates in the capital markets. Locating it in the IMF was considered inappropriate because of the fundamental differences in approach and because of the inability of the IMF to increase its resources by borrowing from the private capital market. The tendency for Stabex to act as an aid agency and its limited coverage to certain African, Caribbean and Pacific countries made it equally unsuitable.

The World Bank was also considered to be inappropriate as it had not paid sufficient attention to the commodity instability problem. The Expert Group considered the proposed Common Fund to be the best place for siting the facility, where it could operate as a third window with its own paid-in capital and callable capital. The Common

Fund was selected as it is a specialized institution dealing with commodity problems and the operation of the facility would fit in well with that of its own. However, the Common Fund was not yet in operation and if there was an inordinate delay in bringing it about, the Expert Group recommended that the facility be located in the World Bank where it could operate as a special window.

The basic features of the UNCTAD facility are given in Table 8.2. Based on these features, the Expert Group presented estimates of the shortfalls in the earnings from the export of primary commodities and of the compensations required. It also carried out simulation exercises on the operations of the UNCTAD facility for the periods 1977-81 and 1986-90. The quantitative features of the UNCTAD facility used for these simulation exercises are also given in Table 8.2

Table 8.3 shows the shortfalls and compensations of the UNCTAD facility for the 1977-82 period, calculated on the basis of the quantitative features listed in Table 8.2. The shortfalls and compensations for the IMF-CFF and Stabex are also given for comparative purposes. It can be seen that the shortfalls and compensations under the UNCTAD scheme ($47.4 billion and $23.7 billion) are much greater than those under the IMF-CFF ($11.9 billion and $7.3 billion) and Stabex ($1.3 billion and $0.8 billion).

The sizes of the shortfalls and the compensations contribute very importantly to the costs of operating a compensatory financing facility. Other determinants include the gross disbursements of the scheme and the cash flow of repayments by recipient countries, the borrowing and lending interest rates, the debt/equity ratio and the extent of concessionality recommended by the Expert Group.

The results of the simulation exercises on the operations of the UNCTAD facility for 1977-81, based on the features recommended by the Expert Group, are given in Tables 8.4 and 8.5. They show that by 1981, the fifth year of operation, the outstanding debt of the facility with the financial markets would be $13.8 billion. The total assets would be $18.8 billion, which consists of $17.1 billion worth of debt from the borrowing developing countries and $1.7 billion worth of investment. The net worth of the facility would be $5 billion, which exceeds the initial capital of $3.5 billion. The facility would thus be financially viable and would remain so as long as its subsidies to the recipient countries are less than the special annual interest subsidy received and the interest earned from its investment performance.

The governments of the member countries, presumably developed ones, would need to contribute not only the $3.5 billion of paid-in capital but also provide callable capital or guarantee of $13.8 billion, to

Table 8.2: Summary of the basic features of the UNCTAD facility

Features		Recommendation of the Expert Group for the main features of the facility	Quantitative features used in the illustrative simulations
A	**Basis for compensatory loans**		
1	Country eligibility	All developing countries	134 developing countries
2	Commodity eligibility	All primary commodities (SITC 0+1+2+4+68)	29 commodities
3	Eligibility for loans	A shortfall according to the formula in a commodity sector	
a	Shortfall formula	Based on an exponential or linear trend value over a ten-year period in nominal terms	Exponential trend value
b	Thresholds	Application of dependency and fluctuation thresholds, both set at 5 per cent	*idem*
4	Size of loans		
a	Compen-sation rate	Not predetermined. It would depend, *inter alia*, on the diagnosis of the causes of the commodity sector shortfalls, and on the multi-year commodity stabilization programme as agreed between the facility and the recipient country.	Average rate of compensation of 50 per cent
b	Basis for the calculation of total loans	Sum of the loans as calculated above in each affected commodity sector (i.e. gross basis)	*idem*
B	**Main operational characteristics**		
5	Lending		
a	Lending policy	Loans will be based on a multi-year commodity stabilization programme as agreed between the facility and the recipient country	

(continued over)

Table 8.2 (continued)

	Features	Recommendation of the Expert Group for the main features of the facility	Quantitative features used in the illustrative simulations
	b Lending terms	Lending interest rate would be based, *inter alia*, on the cost of funds to the facility and on its own borrowing rate	Lending rate at 2 per cent below market rate
		Repayments with a fixed maturity and accelerated repayments whenever surpluses reach a predetermined level	2-year grace period and repayments of principal in 10 equal annual instalments
6	Concessionality for the least developed countries and other low-income countries	Possibility of lower thresholds, higher compensation rate, grants, longer grace period, lower interest rates, greater access to technical assistance. Subsidization of interest rate will only be made to the extent agreed by governments and will be financed through a special interest rate subsidy account	Thresholds = 2 per cent Compensation rate = 75 per cent Grace period = 4 years Interest rate = 0 per cent (applied to least developed countries)
7	Borrowings		
	a Borrowing policy	Borrowings will be the main sources of funds of the facility, which should therefore be managed in a commercial way to secure market support. Most borrowings will be long and medium-term at competitive market rates	Borrowings with an average 2-year grace period and repayment in 10 years
	b Limit on borrowings	Debt less than or equal to callable capital + cumulated net income	*idem*
8	Relations with other facilities		
	a Co-operation	Based on formal co-operation agreements	

(continued over)

Table 8.2 (continued)

Features		Recommendation of the Expert Group for the main features of the facility	Quantitative features used in the illustrative simulations
	b Avoidance of double compensation	The facility will consider the other facilities' drawings in relation to a commodity, as well as additional export earnings of that commodity, in its own calculations	A global average rate of compensation of 50 per cent was considered sufficient protection in assessing the additional resources needed for an additional facility, avoiding double compensation
9	Sources of fund	The facility is to function as a self-financed, commercially managed entity. Its main sources of funds are the paid-in capital, cash generated by its operations, repayment of loans (which will reconstitute its resources), and borrowings in financial markets	*idem*
C	**Capital Structure**		
10	Special accounts		
	a Special interest rate subsidy account	To finance the reduced interest rate to countries eligible for concessionality. Funded by voluntary contributions	
	b Special technical assistance account	To finance technical assistance to countries eligible for concessionality. Funded by voluntary contributions	
11	Total capital		
	a Ratio of paid-in to total capital	A minimum of 1:5	1:5
	b Distribution of government contributions to the paid-in capital	Along the lines of that of the Common Fund for Commodities	

Source: UNCTAD (1985), Annex XI, pp. 7-9.

Table 8.3: Shortfalls and compensation of various compensatory financing facilities, 1977-82.

Compensatory financing facilities		1977-82
IMF-CFF[1]	Shortfalls ($ billion)	11.89
	Compensations ($ billion)	7.34
	Average compensation rate (%)	61.73
	Number of drawings	173
Stabex[2]	Shortfalls ($ billion)	1.34
	Compensations ($ billion)	0.79
	Average compensation rate (%)	58.95
	Number of drawings	129
UNCTAD	Shortfalls ($ billion)	47.42
	Compensations ($ billion)	23.69
	Average compensation rate (%)	50.00
	Number of drawings	471

Source: UNCTAD (1985), Annex XI, p. 6.

[1] The shortfalls and compensations are often calculated for twelve-month periods which do not necessarily coincide with calendar years. In order to obtain figures which are comparable with those of the other two facilities, the shortfalls and compensations were allocated to calendar years on a pro rata basis.
[2] The data cover the ACP states and the EEC member states' overseas territories, including for 1981 the transfers financed by the EEC's extra-budgetary resources.

enable the UNCTAD facility to borrow $13.8 billion from the financial markets. As the operation would be a new one with its clients being mainly poor and economically unstable developing countries, it is highly unlikely that the size of the callable capital could be any smaller.

These figures show that the operation of the UNCTAD facility over the period 1977-81 would require a great deal more financial resources than used for the operation of the IMF-CFF and Stabex, which were $4.2 billion and $0.7 billion respectively. Even if the operation of the UNCTAD facility were to be limited to the least developed countries, the resources required would still amount to $2.6 billion.

The simulation exercises on the operation of the UNCTAD facility for the period 1986-90 show that paid-in capital of $4.4 billion was required with callable capital of $17.7 billion as a guarantee for

Table 8.4: Basic elements of the balance sheet of the UNCTAD facility: illustrative simulation for the period 1977-81[1]

(millions of dollars)

	1976	1977	1978	1979	1980	1981
A Assets						
Investment[2]	3456	1728	1728	1728	1728	1728
Special investment account[3]	186	204	213	188	125	-
Loans (outstanding)		2105	4783	7339	10758	17113
		4038	6724	9255	12611	18841
B Liabilities						
Debt[4]		32	2371	4609	7728	13823
Paid-in capital	3456	3456	3456	3456	3456	3456
Net income[5]		346	684	1002	1301	1562
Special subsidy account	186	204	213	188	125	-
		4038	6724	9255	12611	18841
Basic capital structure						
Total capital	17280					
Paid-in capital	3456					
Callable capital	13824					
Subsidy[3] (paid as a lump-sum)	186					

Source: UNCTAD (1985), Annex XI, p. 10.

1 The specific hypotheses for the period 1977-81 are:
- the average borrowing rate of the facility equals 10 per cent;
- the facility borrows from and lends to the market at the same rate (i.e. there are no "liquidity costs").

2 It is assumed for simplicity that the facility will maintain for the end of each year a minimum level of highly liquid investments equal to one half of its paid-in capital.

3 The special investment account, and its revenue, are intended to finance the special interest rate concessionality to the least developed countries (i.e. 0 per cent). Everything therefore happens as if those countries were subject to the lending rate applied to the other countries (i.e. 8 per cent). Unused funds of the subsidy account are invested in the market at the prevailing interest rate.

4 The debt of the facility at the end of the period is equal to the callable capital. At the end of the period, therefore, the facility would not have exhausted its borrowing capacity (limited by the callable capital plus net income).

5 These figures do not take into account the administrative expenses of the facility and should be adjusted downward. Net income = interest on (investment + loans - borrowed funds) + subsidy account transfers.

Table 8.5: Simulation of the operations of the UNCTAD facility, 1977-81

(millions of dollars)

	1976	1977	1978	1979	1980	1981
A Operations with recipient countries						
1 Cash flows with countries						
Shortfalls		4112	5066	5211	7215	13430
Compensatory loans		2105	2677	2752	3839	7021
Payments by countries:		-	157	532	926	1390
Repayments of principal		-	-	196	420	666
Interest payments		-	157	336	505	723
Net cash outflows		2105	2521	2220	2913	5631
2 Net situation with countries						
Outstanding debt		2105	4783	7339	10758	17113
Subsidy (cumulative):		-	54	201	450	847
Developing countries (in general)[1]		-	42	142	303	548
Least developed countries[2]		-	12	59	147	299
B Sources and uses of the facility funds						
1 Uses of funds (cumulative)						
Disbursements on compensatory loans		2105	4782	7534	11373	18395
Repayments of borrowed funds		-	-	3	240	701
Investment	3456	1728	1728	1728	1728	1728
Special investment account	186	204	213	188	125	-
		4038	6724	9454	13467	20824
2 Sources of funds (cumulative)						
Special interest subsidy account	186	204	213	188	125	-
Resources provided by the paid-in capital	3456	3456	3456	3456	3456	3456
Net income		346	684	1002	1301	1562
Repayment of compensatory loans		-	-	196	616	1282
Borrowings		32	2371	4612	7969	14524
		4038	6724	9454	13467	20824
C Operations with the financial markets						
1 Cash flows with the financial markets lenders						
Annual borrowings		2	2339	2241	3357	6556

(continued over)

Table 8.5 (continued)

	1976	1977	1978	1979	1980	1981
Payments to the financial markets lenders:		-	3	240	698	1235
Repayment of principal		-	-	3	237	461
Interest payments		-	3	237	461	773
Net cash inflows		32	2336	2001	2659	5321
2 Net situation with the financial markets						
Outstanding debt		32	2371	4609	7728	13823
Investment		1932	1941	1916	1853	1728

Source: UNCTAD (1985), Annex XI, p. 11.

[1] Subsidy due to the small interest rate differential (2 per cent) between the market rate and the lending rate to developing countries in general.

[2] Subsidy due to the 0 per cent interest rate granted to the least developed countries (as compared to the interest rate charged to developing countries in general.)

borrowing the same amount from the financial markets. The outstanding debt would still be $3.5 billion even if the operation was limited to the least developed countries. Again these figures show that the operation of the proposed UNCTAD facility would require resources which exceed anything contemplated for the operation of the IMF-CFF and Stabex.

9
Is There a Need for a New Facility?

Views of Countries and International Organizations on the UNCTAD Facility

The report of the Expert Group on compensating financing of shortfalls in export earnings was published in early 1985. At its meeting to discuss this report, the Trade and Development Board of UNCTAD took three decisions. First, it invited all member-states, the regional commissions of the United Nations (e.g. the Economic Commission for Latin America and the Caribbean) and "competent" international organizations (e.g. the World Bank) to provide written comments on the report. Second, it set up an Intergovernmental Group of Experts to continue the analysis on the need for a new compensatory financing facility and on the rules and modalities of such a facility. Third, it requested the UNCTAD Secretariat to help the new study-group by providing its comments on the report of the Expert Group.

The Secretary-General of UNCTAD wrote to all the parties concerned in August 1985 for views on the report of the Expert Group. This was followed by a reminder note in early December 1985. By the time the Intergovernmental Group of Experts met for the first time in July 1986, seventeen member-states had responded. Eight of these were developing countries (Angola, Chile, Cuba, Ecuador, Iraq, Peru, Qatar and Sri Lanka) and nine developed ones (Denmark, Finland, Italy, Japan, Norway, Sweden, United Kingdom, USSR and West Germany). None of the eight developing countries had submitted views to the Expert Group on compensatory financing, whereas five of the developed ones (Finland, Italy, Norway, Sweden and West Germany) had done so.

There were four submissions from regional commissions of the United Nations (Latin America and the Caribbean, Western Asia, Asia and the Pacific, and Africa) and six from international organizations (World Bank, IMF, the Inter-American Development Bank, the International Cocoa Organization, the European Community and the International Tin Council).

The views of the seventeen member-countries, the four United Nations' regional commissions and the six international organizations on the Expert Group's report are summarized in Table 9.1. Among the developing countries, Angola, Ecuador, Iraq and Peru supported the Expert Group's recommendation very strongly, while Chile and Qatar argued that the most realistic and concrete approach would be to improve the existing machinery. Cuba and Sri Lanka did not commit themselves either way. No developed country came out supporting the scheme. Italy, Japan, the United Kingdom and West Germany were against it, all making the point that substantial facilities already exist to assist countries recovering from shortfalls in export earnings and that the best way forward is to improve such facilities and not create a new compensatory financing facility. The four Scandinavian countries were non-committal, as was the USSR.

Of the four regional commissions of the United Nations, only one (Africa) supported the Expert Group's recommendation, the other three being non-committal. The response from the International Tin Council was also neutral. The IMF did not respond directly to the request for comments on the UNCTAD facility. It agreed that supply factors were important in causing instability in export earnings and also with the observation that its own scheme dealt only with the effects of supply instability on countries' balance-of-payments. However, it did not say whether it supported or rejected the proposal.

The Council and Commission of the European Communities submitted a carefully worded response. It commented on the high quality of the report and generally tried to maintain a neutral stance. However, it eventually came to the conclusion that the possibilities provided by the existing schemes should be studied more specifically and thoroughly. Reading in between the lines, it probably came out against the scheme.

There was no such hesitation on the part of the World Bank. It saw instability in export earnings as only one aspect of the development problem and believed that any attempt to isolate it for special treatment as misguided. It then argued that its development programmes, if balanced and co-ordinated, would have adequately taken into account instability issues. It ended its submission by stating that the case for a new facility had not been convincingly established.

In addition to the responses from seventeen member-states, four

Table 9.1: Views of countries and international organizations on UNCTAD facility, 1986

For	Against	Neutral
Angola, Ecuador, Iraq, Peru	Chile, Qatar	Cuba, Sri Lanka
	West Germany, Japan, Italy, UK	Denmark, Finland, Norway, Sweden, USSR
Inter-American Development Bank (IADB)	World Bank	Economic Commission for Latin America and the Caribbean (ECLAC)
International Cocoa Organization Secretariat (ICCO)		Council and Commission of the European Communities
Economic Commission for Africa (ECA)		Economic and Social Commission for Western Asia (ESCWA)
		Economic and Social Commission for Asia and the Pacific (ESCAP)
		International Monetary Fund (IMF)
		International Tin Council Secretariat (ITC)

Source: UNCTAD (7 April 1986, 5 May 1986 and 6 June 1986).

regional commissions of the United Nations and six international organizations, the Intergovernmental Group of Experts also had a report by the UNCTAD Secretariat (UNCTAD, 1986b). This pointed out that the experiences of the IMF-CFF and Stabex supported the finding of the Expert Group that supply factors are a principal source of instability in export earnings at the country-level. It estimated that, using the Expert Group's proposals, the average annual shortfall in export earnings was $9 billion over the period 1978-83. The annual sum spent by the IMF-CFF and Stabex and by the World Bank on the commodities eligible under the Expert Group scheme was only $1.7 billion, and only a limited part of this was in programmes to reduce supply instability at the sectoral level.

The UNCTAD Secretariat concluded that the existing multilateral facilities were not suitable for dealing with supply instability problems at the commodity-sector level. It agreed with the Expert Group that there is a need for an additional facility to tackle the root causes of supply instability and that such a facility be established as a third window of the Common Fund.

Views of the Intergovernmental Group of Experts

When this group met in July 1986 it therefore had conflicting views on the recommendation of the Expert Group for a new compensatory financing facility. It was also aware that the government of the USA, the most important potential contributor to the scheme, was very much against the proposal, even though it did not put in a submission.

The Intergovernmental Group of Experts agreed with the general observation that shortfalls caused by instability in commodity export earnings have "severe impacts" on the social and economic development of many developing countries (UNCTAD, 1986e). It also agreed that as the shortfalls constrain the ability of those countries to service their debts and to import, they would also be of concern to the international community. It then observed that the shortfalls were caused by supply and demand and related factors.

The committee was not prepared to commit itself further and agreed that it required more information. It therefore requested the UNCTAD Secretariat, in co-operation with the IMF, the World Bank and the Commission of the European Communities, to (i) calculate the shortfalls in export earnings using different formulas and reference periods and on a gross and net basis in US dollars and SDR; (ii) provide information on the extent to which such shortfalls have been covered by the existing international facilities, together with an analysis of the limitations of such facilities; and (iii) assess the impact that shortfalls have on the economic development of developing countries.

Very little was achieved in the July 1986 meeting as far as the rejection or acceptance of the Expert Group's report was concerned. What was agreed was couched in very general terms and, when considered in relation to the request to the UNCTAD Secretariat for more data and analysis, was quite meaningless. For example, the agreement that export instability has severe impacts on social and economic development meant nothing as the group then asked the UNCTAD Secretariat to assess the effect of instability on development.

In many ways the result was expected. The committee was an intergovernmental one with its members representing their governments' views on the need for an additional compensatory financing facility. They could not represent their own views, unlike the case of the members of the Expert Group, who were appointed in their own right as experts on compensatory financing. In view of the diverse views expressed by governments on the need for a new compensatory financing scheme, it is not surprising that the Intergovernmental Group of Experts was not able to come to any far-reaching conclusions at its first meeting.

The second session of the group was held in September 1987 and had before it the study requested from the UNCTAD Secretariat. It agreed that most developing countries had sizeable shortfalls in their commodity export earnings and that these exceeded very substantially the finance currently available for compensating them (UNCTAD, 1987) In contrast to its non-committal position in the first session, the group agreed that shortfalls have a severe negative impact on the social and economic development of these countries, especially the least developed ones, and saw the issue as one of concern for the world.

However, that was as far as it could go and what followed was a play for time. The group noted that the IMF was reviewing the operation of its compensatory financing facility and considered it inappropriate for any recommendations on the report of the Expert Group to be made before the IMF had completed its review. It therefore proposed that the second session be resumed in 1988 and requested the IMF to supply it with the results of any study on the impact that proposed changes to the IMF-CFF would have on compensating shortfalls. It also asked the UNCTAD Secretariat to continue its analytical work on the issue.

The resumed second session took place in April 1989. It did not make any more progress in its deliberations on the Expert Group's report (UNCTAD, 1989). However, the meeting did enable various groupings of countries within UNCTAD to express their vastly different views on the substantive recommendations of the Expert Group.

Thus the Group of 77 (a group of developing countries within UNCTAD, originally numbering 77), supported by China, argued for setting up a new compensatory financing facility. It felt that the replacement of the IMF-CFF in August 1988 by the IMF's Compensatory and Contingency Financing Facility (IMF-CCFF) did not help matters much as far as tackling the root causes of supply instability was concerned. The compensatory financing element of the new facility was essentially the same as that of the old scheme. Moreover, the quota limits were reduced and specific requirements for countries with balance-of-payments difficulties were included, whereas the quota limits should have been increased and the degree of conditionality reduced.

In their support for a new compensatory financing scheme, the Group of 77 recommended that it be set up with a number of principles. First, it should be open to all developing countries and cover all primary commodities. Second, there should be low or no conditionality, with funds to be disbursed relatively automatically and quickly. Third, the interest rates charged should be low and the repayment period long to take into account a country's capacity to repay. Fourth, special provisions should be made for the least developed countries, especially African ones. Fifth, the funds should be used for solving the problems of instability in the commodity sector and should also encourage processing and diversification in it.

As an intermediate measure, the Group of 77 recommended that a multilaterally agreed set of principles, objectives, rules and modalities for the operation of existing and forthcoming compensatory financing schemes be established. The principles listed previously were to be given priority.

The views of the Group of 77 were opposed diametrically by the countries of Group B, made up of the major Western industrial nations and Japan. They argued that the need had not been established for either an additional compensatory financing facility or a multilaterally agreed set of principles, objectives, rules and modalities. They also pointed out that it was too early to pass judgment on the workings of the IMF-CCFF.

In view of such major differences in the positions of two groups of countries, the Intergovernmental Group of Experts could only conclude that the problem of export instability and the actions taken or to be taken by international organizations in dealing with it should be kept under continuous review by UNCTAD and other bodies.

Framework of Evaluation

It can be seen from the submissions to the Expert Group and from the submissions to the Intergovernmental Group of Experts that the views of governments on the need for an additional compensatory financing facility differ very markedly. The views of international organizations also differ significantly.

It can also be seen that most of the views on the recommendation of the Expert Group for an additional compensatory financing facility have been derived without the use of an explicit evaluative framework. This makes it difficult, if not impossible, to identify the basis or reason for the acceptance or rejection of the proposal. In this section a framework for evaluation is developed, which is then used for assessing the Expert Group's recommendation.

The Expert Group's recommendation for an additional compensatory financing facility, whose funds are to be used for adjusting supply in specific commodity sectors, is based on a number of sequential arguments. Whether or not the proposal can be supported depends on two considerations. The first is the validity of each of the arguments, the second the extent to which these arguments have been linked together in a logical and consistent way.

As the Expert Group's recommendation is built on a number of sequential points, its case will be damaged if only one of the arguments cannot be sustained. The whole case is only as strong as the weakest link in the chain. Moreover, even if each and every one of the arguments were to be valid, it is still possible to end up with a *non sequitur* and an indefensible overall position.

The various arguments and the sequence in which they appear have been presented by the Expert Group in the following way. First, it points out that many developing countries have a high and a sustained level of instability in their export earnings. Second, it argues that this instability is harmful to the economic growth of the primary-producing sectors, the developing countries and the world as a whole. Third, it shows that while instability in export earnings is caused by both demand and supply factors, the latter are more important at the country level. Fourth, this then suggests that to deal effectively with instability, policy measures should be directed at the factors which cause supply instability at the sectoral level.

Fifth, the Expert Group argues that the existing compensatory financing facilities do not deal adequately with the root causes of supply instability at the sectoral level. Thus the IMF-CFF aims only to stabilize export earnings rather than deal with the factors which produce the instability, Stabex operates in reality as an aid agency and the World Bank, while it could deal with the causes of supply instability, has not seen export instability as a serious developmental problem.

Sixth, there is therefore a need for a new compensatory facility which uses its funds for programmes which reduce supply uncertainty in specific primary commodity sectors, in ways which are consistent with national and international policies and arrangements. Lastly, the new facility is to be located in the Common Fund in view of the latter's concern for primary commodities. If the Common Fund were not to become operational within a reasonable time, the new facility should be operated as a separate "window" in the World Bank.

According to the framework proposed for assessing the Expert Group's compensatory financing scheme, two questions have to be asked. First, how valid is each of the seven arguments presented? Second, how does each argument logically flow on to the next to produce a sustainable overall position?

Assessment of the UNCTAD Facility

There is general agreement that developing countries as a whole experience more fluctuations in their export earnings than developed countries. On balance, the academic literature and the experiences of national governments and international organizations which have to deal with export instability suggest that such instability is detrimental to economic growth. It can also be argued that, on balance, supply factors are more important than demand ones in explaining instability in export earnings at the country level.

Once these three points have been conceded, then it follows that, to reduce instability in export earnings and to lessen its adverse impact on economic growth on a permanent basis, policy measures have indeed to be targeted at the factors which cause supply instability at the sectoral level. The case for having such an approach to the export instability issue is made.

However, the case for having an additional compensatory financing facility along the lines recommended by the Expert Group is less clear. While it is undoubtedly true that the IMF-CFF and Stabex deal only with the effects of export instability and that the World

Bank's structural adjustment programmes see instability as only one of many development problems, this does not necessarily mean that the case for the UNCTAD facility is automatically made.

First, the Expert Group's recommendation that compensatory financing be used for setting up marketing boards and domestic loan schemes to stabilize the prices and incomes of primary producers at the national level can be criticized. If there are government policies which increase price and income instability, then the answer is to eliminate such policies. It is not to create yet more government bodies to deal with the original offending policies. Also, the experience of marketing boards in Africa suggests that these will be used not primarily to stabilize prices and incomes, but to extract resources from the primary sector. The pursuit of this disguised form of a negative agricultural price policy will reduce agricultural output in the long run.

Second, the case for using scarce development funds for compensating export shortfalls for countries with fluctuating but healthy balance-of-payments can be questioned. In any case, these countries will most likely be able to introduce built-in stabilizers to even the fluctuations if they saw a need for them. The UNCTAD proposal is vague on the conditions under which countries can draw on the additional facility.

Third, in essence, most of the programmes that have been identified as necessary to partially or wholly eliminate the causes of supply instability are ones that would be contained in any structural adjustment programme. For example, the programme to ensure greater reliability in the supply of key production inputs, especially imported ones, would be an important part of a broadly-based bigger plan to increase the efficiency and the growth potential of the primary sector concerned. The latter would also be concerned with the diversification of the production base of the country, in order to reduce the degree of commodity concentration but taking care that the new commodities chosen have good long-term prospects. The result of a successful structural adjustment programme would be greater stability and growth in the export sector.

The essential difference then between the UNCTAD proposal and a normal structural adjustment programme is that the former would deal exclusively with reducing supply instability and the harmful effects instability has on economic growth, while the latter would include the instability issue as part of a bigger balanced and co-ordinated programme.

If export instability is seen as an integral part of the general problem of a lack of economic development, then a co-ordinated programme of action would be preferred to one which deals only with the instability issue. Given this, the type of structural adjustment programme envisaged looks suspiciously like the structural and sectoral adjustment programmes of the World Bank.

These are designed to increase the competitiveness of a country's export sector by changing its trade regime, mobilizing its domestic and foreign resources, improving the efficiency of domestic resource use and bringing about institutional reforms. The programme was begun in 1980 and was reinforced, for those countries which have demonstrated willingness to introduce economic reforms, by the introduction of the Special Action Programme in 1983.

It would, however, be true to say that the World Bank has not taken the issue of export instability seriously enough. Its major concern has been on what it considers to be the more important issue, the strong growth of the export sector, in spite of its declared interest in, and concern for, the detrimental effects of export instability. As noted earlier, the World Bank's first specific involvement with the problem of instability came with its proposal in 1965 to establish a supplementary facility to the IMF-CFF. This was in response to an UNCTAD request for a study on the matter, and differs importantly from the IMF-CFF in not tying its help to a balance-of-payments need. It was to be located in the World Bank but operated in consultation with the IMF.

This proposal did not get very far because very few developed countries were prepared to supply the additional funds needed. It is also a proposal that the World Bank has never returned to. For the rest of the 1960s, the World Bank, together with the IMF, carried out studies on the methods of price stabilization. This work culminated in the set of decisions it took in 1969 to finance agricultural diversification, and research and development projects.

In 1978 a joint World Bank and IMF report on the stabilization of export earnings appeared and was revised in 1979 (IMF-World Bank, 1979). This proposed that temporary shortfalls in export earnings should continue to be dealt by the IMF-CFF, but only after improving that facility. For shortfalls that are not temporary, financial assistance from the World Bank for a medium-term structural adjustment programme can be obtained through programme lending.

As a result of the joint study, the compensation base of the IMF-CFF was expanded in 1979 to include workers' remittances and income from tourism. The limit on drawings was raised to 100 per cent of the quota and the constraint on drawings in any twelve-month period was removed. The current method of estimating the trend in export earnings was also introduced in that year.

In spite of such a background of involvement in development issues related to export instability, the specific instances where the World Bank has given loans to offset export shortfalls have been rare. Most of these had been made prior to 1980, since when practically all programme lending has been for structural adjustment predicated by balance-of-payments difficulties. The making of this observation does not mean that the World Bank cannot be persuaded that developing countries need strong and stable growth in exports or that its structural and sectoral adjustment programmes cannot be designed in future to pay more attention to the instability issue.

To conclude, while the case for having a different approach to export instability is made, that for having a new compensatory financing facility is less certain. The reality of the situation may also make the operation of such a facility, were it to be established, difficult. Those countries which have export instability, and take its impact seriously, as well as balance-of-payments difficulties, would remain with the IMF because of the subsidized operation of its compensatory element and use the drawings to deal with the causes of supply instability. Those that have unstable export earnings and constant balance-of-payments difficulties would naturally be more concerned with the latter and seek World Bank soft loans. Those that have unstable export earnings and no balance-of-payments difficulties would have no incentive to turn to the new facility as its loans can be obtained only at commercial rates, and the countries concerned have easy access to existing international capital markets.

The case for establishing the UNCTAD facility is weakened further by the replacement, in August 1988, of the IMF's Compensatory Financing Facility (IMF-CFF) by its Compensatory and Contingency Financing Facility (IMF-CCFF). The new facility retains the compensatory financing element of the old scheme but also provides contingency funds to developing countries whose macroeconomic and structural adjustment programmes, introduced to eliminate protracted balance-of-payments problems, are threatened by external economic shocks. This new contingency element seems to possess many of the features of the UNCTAD facility.

The IMF's Compensatory and Contingency Financing Facility (IMF-CCFF)

The compensating arm of the IMF-CCFF operates in the same way as the IMF-CFF. The only major changes are in the formula used for calculating the size of the shortfall in export earnings and the introduction of a procedure to avoid over-compensation in successive purchases when the projections of export earnings underlying an earlier drawing are over-optimistic (Pownall and Stuart, 1988).

The contingency arm of the new scheme provides funds to maintain the momentum of macroeconomic and structural adjustment in the face of adverse economic external shocks (Cheney, undated). Such adjustment programmes are introduced to deal with severe and prolonged balance-of-payments deficits brought about by a country's own bad economic decisions. The momentum of these programmes can be halted by adverse movements in important external economic factors. By providing funds to cover deviations in some of these key economic variables from "baseline" forecasts, the contingency financing element can reduce the vulnerability of a country's adjustment programmes, increase the country's confidence to adopt the longer-term economic measures needed to deal with serious and deeply embedded economic problems and ultimately help it to achieve sustained economic growth.

Thus, unlike the compensatory mechanism, the contingency mechanism provides funds to counter economic instability only when adjustment programmes are taking place and when the success of such programmes is threatened by unexpected external economic changes. By insisting that adjustment and contingency financing programmes go hand in hand, the contingency element ensures that funds would be made available only to countries which have protracted balance-of-payments problems and which are seriously doing something about them. It also ensures that, unlike the UNCTAD facility, countries with healthy though unstable balance-of-payments would not be entitled to scarce funds. The contingency element of the IMF-CCFF thus sees export instability as only a part, though an important one, of the general problem of economic underdevelopment. It deals with the root causes of supply instability by insisting that macroeconomic and structural adjustment programmes are carried out. Instability in key external economic variables, which produces instability in the balance-of-payments through the current account side, is dealt with by the provision of contingency funding.

The key external economic variables are export prices, import prices, interest rates, worker remittances and tourism earnings. Deviations in these from the "baseline" forecasts must be due to factors beyond the control of the member-country. Changes in capital movements and in the volume of imported goods and services are not covered nor are the consequences of natural disasters.

The range of unforeseen external disruptions under the IMF-CCFF is thus broader than that under the IMF-CFF. The inclusion of unexpected increases in international interest rates is particularly innovative. This provision reduces the threat that large increases in interest rates and the resulting increase in the burden of interest payments on foreign debt have on the adjustment programmes of countries that have borrowed on variable interest rates.

Contingency funding is available to countries which are undertaking different types of adjustment programmes. The first is the "stand-by arrangement", where a one-to-three-year line of credit is provided to fund a one-to-three-year programme of economic and financial adjustment to correct balance-of-payments problems. The second is the "extended Fund facility" arrangement, where credit with a longer repayment period is available to support a three-year economic and financial adjustment programme which includes structural changes. The third is a programme under the "structural adjustment facility", where concessional funding is made available to low-income developing countries carrying out a three-year economic and structural adjustment programme. The fourth is a programme under the "enhanced structural adjustment facility", which provides credit under essentially the same terms as the "structural adjustment facility" but for the pursuit of more ambitious objectives. It should be noted that countries with adjustment programmes under the "structural adjustment facility" and the "enhanced structural adjustment facility" are eligible for contingency financing only if their adjustment programmes qualify them for funds under the stand-by or extended arrangements.

When contingency financing is approved by the IMF's Executive Board, it is done so with all the details, including the external variables covered, the "baseline" forecasts used and the method for calculating the amount of contingency financing, clearly specified. A country can draw on the contingency funds when it is faced with unanticipated deviations from the "baseline" forecasts for the key external variables concerned, usually estimated for between twelve and eighteen months. The amount of contingency finance available is calculated as the net negative effect of such deviations on the country's balance-of-payments. However, this amount must exceed a minimum threshold amount to ensure that only major balance-of-payments deficits are covered. Normally this threshold is equal to 10 per cent of the country's quota, or financial contribution, in the IMF.

If the threshold criterion is satisfied, an amount equal to 4 per cent of the country's quota has to be deducted from the net amount of contingency financing. This is imposed as the country is expected to be able to provide such a cushioning effect on its own. A further deduction is then made as only a specified percentage of the net amount less the 4 per cent deduction is granted by the IMF-CCFF. This percentage is determined on a case-by-case basis and is expected to be high in the early stages of the adjustment programme.

The amount of funds available to a country under the IMF-CCFF is limited to 122 per cent of the country's quota in the IMF. This is divided into 40 per cent for the compensatory financing of shortfalls in export earnings, 40 per cent for financing large increases in the cost of cereal imports and an optional 25 per cent to be used, at the country's choice, to supplement any of the above three.

If a country applies only for compensatory finance to deal with either export shortfalls or excesses in the cost of cereal imports, the access is limited to the previous level of 83 per cent of quota or a combined limit of 105 per cent.

There are additional ceilings for contingency financing. It cannot exceed 70 per cent of the funds spent by the IMF on the adjustment programme to which the contingency element is attached. For IMF-supported adjustment programmes which last for more than one year, the amount of contingency financing available to a country "may normally not exceed 70 per cent of the annual amount available from the IMF under the associated arrangement" (Cheney, undated:10). There is also a separate cumulative sub-limit of 35 per cent of quota on contingency financing for unexpected increases in international interest rates.

In order to understand better the ways in which these entries are brought into play, it would be useful to work through a hypothetical case of contingency financing. The example is taken from Cheney (undated).

A developing country has a protracted balance-of-payments problem and a large foreign debt. It has adopted a one-year adjustment programme to deal with this. The programme is supported by the IMF through its stand-by arrangement with financing of SDR 50 million. The country's quota, or subscription in the IMF, is SDR 90 million. The provision of the funds is subject to the country introducing certain policies to deal with its balance-of-payments problem.

The country is very dependent on the export of primary commodities, especially coffee, whose prices are very unstable and on earnings from tourism. At the same time a large part of its substantial foreign debt consists of borrowing on variable interest rates. The country's adjustment programme is thus very vulnerable to external economic factors which are outside its control. It therefore requests that the programme be protected by contingency financing from the unforeseen and adverse effects of rising interest rates, falling coffee prices and decreasing earnings from tourism.

The Executive Board of the IMF agrees to the provision of contingency financing. The external economic variables covered are interest rates, export prices for coffee and earnings from tourism. The "baseline" forecast for interest rates over the year of the adjustment programme is an increase of half of one percentage point, while the export prices for coffee are expected to rise by 5 per cent and earnings from tourism to remain constant.

The impact of deviations of the three key variables from these "baseline" forecasts on the country's balance-of-payments is the combined effect of three adverse movements. The first is the increase in the interest rate greater than the projected increase of half of one percentage point, multiplied by the amount of the country's foreign debt that carries variable interest rates. The second is the adverse movement in coffee export prices relative to the projected 5 per cent increase, multiplied by the export volume specified in the contingency financing programme. The third is the adverse movement in tourism earnings.

Eight months after the start of the adjustment and contingency financing programme, world interest rates increased by 3 percentage points in excess of the "baseline" forecast. This resulted in an increase in the country's foreign debt service payment by SDR 36 million. The prices of coffee exports fell by 5 per cent, against the "baseline" forecast of a 5 per cent increase. This resulted in a fall in coffee export earnings of SDR 22.5 million. On the other hand, earnings from tourism went up by 3 per cent, against a forecast of no change, and produced an increase in tourism earnings of SDR 13.5 million.

The net impact of these three movements on the country's balance-of-payments was thus a decrease of SDR 45.0 million. As this amount was 50 per cent of the country's quota in the IMF, it was able to satisfy the threshold criterion. However, the actual amount of contingency financing it could obtain would be less than SDR 45.0 million. First, an amount equal to 4 per cent of the country's quota had to be deducted, which reduced the sum to SDR 41.4 million. Second, the IMF-CCFF provides contingency financing for only a certain percentage of this sum. In this illustration it was 80 per cent, which meant that a sum of SDR 33.12 million was made available.

Contingency financing of this volume was possible as it conformed with two financing guidelines. First, it amounted to 36.8

per cent of the country's quota in the IMF, which is below the permissible level of 40 per cent allowed under the IMF-CCFF for contingency financing. Second, it amounted to 66.2 per cent of the SDR 50 million which the IMF provided for the country's adjustment programme under the stand-by arrangement. This conformed with the guideline that contingency financing in any one year be less than 70 per cent of the financing available for the associated adjustment programme.

Conclusions

In general, developing countries experience significantly greater fluctuations in export earnings than developed countries, largely because they depend more on the export of primary products. The low price elasticities of supply and demand of these products and frequent and large shifts in their supply and demand are adequate reasons for explaining export instability. At the commodity and country level, volume instability appears, on balance, to be more pronounced than price instability, and supply factors more important than demand ones in explaining instability in export earnings.

Export instability can slow down economic growth by reducing investment and encouraging the wrong type of investment, by using up the time of scarce skilled personnel in monitoring it, and by contributing to social and political unrest. After discounting the results of those empirical studies which examined developing countries that cannot *prima facie* be affected by instability, and the results of those which adopted a theoretically incorrect way of testing the hypothesis, the balance of the evidence seems to support the argument that export instability has been detrimental to economic growth. The important international organizations dealing with development certainly believe in the harmful effect of instability on growth.

One of these organizations, the International Monetary Fund, operated a compensatory financing facility (IMF-CFF) for the period 1963-88. This was an important scheme as it accounted for a quarter of the total credit extended by the IMF over that period. However, the facility had not been able to stabilize export earnings because a number of its features acted against that. The effects of a repayment system, which did not insist on repayment whenever there was an export surplus and a favourable balance-of-payments situation, and an unreliable method of calculating the export shortfall were particularly damaging.

Another weakness of the IMF-CFF is that it set out only to stabilize export earnings rather than deal with the factors which produce the instability. To prevent export instability from recurring, it needed to tackle the causes of export instability, which are basically centred on supply uncertainty at the commodity and country level. Demand uncertainty cannot be ignored as a cause of export instability but, as it emanates from uncertainty in demand from developed nations, there are no practical ways of dealing with it.

The facility also linked the provision of compensatory financing to a balance-of-payments need. By so doing, it could effectively have dealt with only one of the many ways in which export instability can harm the process of economic growth. However, in reality this is not a serious criticism.

The Stabex scheme of the European Community functions basically as a vehicle for transferring foreign aid. It does not pretend to stabilize the export earnings of the recipient countries on a temporary or permanent basis.

The case for having an approach to instability which deals with its causes and the entire range of economic problems that it produces is clear. However, the case for having an additional compensatory financing facility, whether located in the proposed Common Fund or the World Bank, is not as clear. In essence, most of the programmes considered necessary to eliminate the causes of supply instability would be contained in any broadly-based plan to increase the efficiency and the growth potential of the commodity sector concerned. The difference between the Expert Group's proposal for an additional facility and a normal structural adjustment programme, such as the World Bank one, is that the former would deal exclusively with reducing supply instability and the harmful effects instability has on growth, while the latter would include the instability issue as one of many problems to be dealt with by a bigger and more balanced and co-ordinated programme aimed at greater economic stability and growth.

If the problem of export instability is seen as an integral part of the general problem of economic underdevelopment, it should be dealt with by a broadly-based programme concerned with promoting greater growth and stability. This argues then not for the establishment of an additional compensatory financing facility but for the World Bank to pay adequate attention to the instability issue in its structural and sectoral adjustment programmes. By raising the instability issue the way they did, UNCTAD and the Expert Group might go some way in persuading the World Bank to accord export instability the importance it deserves. They might have helped, wittingly or unwittingly, those who were successful in replacing, in August 1988, the IMF's Compensatory Financing Facility (IMF-CFF) by its Compensatory and Contingency Financing Facility (IMF-CCFF). It might have helped wittingly in the sense that the thrust of its argument was taken on board and the IMF-CFF changed to take this into account. It might have helped unwittingly in the sense that unless some notice was taken of the thrust of its argument, a new compensatory facility could be established in the long run. The establishment of the IMF-CCFF might not have been first-best but it was much less likely to create distortions in the international economic system than the creation of the UNCTAD facility.

The value of the Expert Group's scheme in this respect could have been enhanced by the relative mildness of its key features when compared to those proposed by the UNCTAD Secretariat (1981). The latter suggested four basic principles on which a new compensatory facility should be based. These were that shortfalls should be measured in real terms and calculated on the basis of a long-term trend; countries should be compensated for the full extent of their shortfalls; no conditions were to be attached to drawings; and terms of repayment and interest charges should be related to the ability of the recipient to repay.

None of these principles, with the exception of the calculation of the shortfalls on the basis of a long-term trend, was accepted by the Expert Group. It argued that the shortfalls be measured in nominal terms; the compensation rate be dependent on a number of factors including the nature of the supply instability; drawings be subjected to dependency and fluctuation thresholds; and the interest rate charged be based on the borrowing rate or the cost of the fund to the facility and not on the ability of the borrowing country to repay.

Bibliography

Adams, F.G. and Behrman, J.R. (1982) *Commodity Exports and Economic Development: The Commodity Problem, Goal Attainment and Policy in Developing Countries*, Lexington, Mass.: Lexington Books, D.C. Heath.

Ariff, K.A.M. (1972) *Export Trade and the West Malaysian Economy: An Enquiry into the Economic Implications of Export Instability*, Kuala Lumpur: University of Malaya, Faculty of Economics and Administration Monographs on Malaysian Economic Development.

Batchelor, R.A., Major, R.L. and Morgan, A.D. (1980) *Industrialisation and the Basis for Trade*, Cambridge: Cambridge University Press.

Bautista, R., Hughes, H., Lim, D., Morawetz, D. and Thoumi, F. (1981) *Capital Utilisation in Manufacturing in Developing Countries*, New York: Oxford University Press.

Behrman, J.R. (1968) *Supply Response in Underdeveloped Agriculture: A Case Study of Four Major Annual Crops in Thailand 1937-1963*, Amsterdam: North Holland Publishing Co.

Brundell, P., Horn, H. and Svedberg, P. (1981) 'On the Causes of Instability in Export Earnings', *Oxford Bulletin of Economics and Statistics* 43, 3:301-313.

Caine, S. (1954) 'Instability of Producers' Incomes: A Protest and a Proposal', *Economic Journal* 64, 255:610-614.

Cheney, D.M. (undated) *Promoting Economic Stability: The IMF's Compensatory and Contingency Financing Facility*, Washington, D.C.: International Monetary Fund.

Commission of the European Communities (1981) *Comprehensive Report of the Export Earnings Stabilization System Established by the Lomé Convention for the Years 1975 to 1979*, Brussels: European Economic Community.

Commission of the European Communities (1985) *Stabex: User's Guide*, Brussels: European Economic Community.

Coppock, J.D. (1962) *International Economic Instability*, New York: McGraw-Hill Publishing Company.

Corden, W.M. (1984) 'Booming Sector and Dutch Disease Economics: Survey and Consolidation', *Oxford Economic Papers* 36, 3:359-380.

Cuddy, J. and Della Valle, P.A. (1978) 'Measuring the Instability of Time Series Data', *Oxford Bulletin of Economics and Statistics* 40, 1:79-84.

Due, J. (1970) *Indirect Taxation in Developing Countries*, Baltimore: Johns Hopkins Press.

Erb, G.F. and Schiavo-Campo, S. (1969) 'Export Instability, Level of Development and Economic Size of Less Developed Countries', *Oxford Bulletin of Economics and Statistics* 31, 4:263-283.

Ezekiel, H. (1985) *The IMF Cereal Import Financing Scheme*, Washington, D.C.: International Food Policy Research Institute.

Finger, J.M. and Derosa, D.A. (1980) 'The Compensatory Finance Facility and Export Instability', *Journal of World Trade Law* 14, 1:14-22.

Glezakos, C. (1973) 'Export Instability and Economic Growth: A Statistical Verification', *Economic Development and Cultural Change* 21, 4:670-678.

Goreux, L.M. (1980) *Compensatory Financing Facility*, Washington, D.C.: International Monetary Fund.

Guillaumont, P. (1987) 'From Export Instability Effects to International Stabilisation Policies', *World Development* 15, 5:633-643.

Herrmann, R. (1982) 'On the Economic Evaluation of the Stabex System', *Intereconomics* 18, 1/2: 7-12.

________ (1983) *The Compensatory Financing System of the International Monetary Fund*, Kiel: Kieler Wissenchaftsverlag Vauk.

Hewitt, A.P. (1983) 'Stabex: An Evaluation of the Economic Impact Over the First Five Years', *World Development* 11,

12:1005-1027.

________ (1987) 'Stabex and Commodity Export Compensation Schemes: Prospects for Globalisation', *World Development* 15, 5:617-631.

Hirschman, A. (1958) *The Strategy of Economic Development*, New Haven: Yale University Press.

Idachaba, F.S. (1975) 'Revenue Instability in Developing Countries: The Ghanaian Experience', *Public Finance*, 30, 1:96-100.

International Monetary Fund (1976-88) *Annual Report*, Washington, D.C.

________ (1984) 'The Compensatory Financing Facility of the IMF: A Report Prepared by the Staff of the International Monetary Fund', in United Nations Conference for Trade and Development (1985) *Compensatory Financing of Export Earnings Shortfall*, New York: United Nations.

________ (1986) 'Fund Experience concerning Export Supply Instability', in UNCTAD (1986a).

________ and the Work Bank (1979) *Stabilization of Export Earnings: A Further Study Prepared by the Staff of the IMF and the World Bank*, Washington, D.C.

Kanbur, S.M.R. (1986) *The Economic Analysis of International Commodity Price Stabilization: A Review*, paper prepared for the FAO, Rome.

Kenen, P. and Voivodas, C. (1972) 'Export Instability and Economic Growth', *Kyklos* 25, 4:791-804.

Knudsen, O. and Parnes, A. (1975) *Trade Instability and Economic Development*, Lexington, Mass.: Lexington Books, D.C. Heath.

________ and Yotopoulos, P. (1976) 'A Transitory Approach to Export Instability', *Food Research Institute Studies* 15, 1:91-108.

Lam, N.V. (1980) 'Export Instability, Expansion and Market Concentration: A Methodological Interpretation', *Journal of Development Economics* 7, 1:99-115.

Lancieri, E. (1978) 'Export Instability and Economic Development: A Reappraisal', *Banca Nazionale del Lavoro Quarterly Review* 125:135-152.

Lawson, C. (1974) 'The Decline in World Export Instability: A Reappraisal', *Oxford Bulletin of Economics and Statistics* 36, 1:53-65.

Leith, J.C. (1970) 'The Decline in World Export Instability: A Comment', *Oxford Bulletin of Economics and Statistics* 32, 2:267-272.

Lim, D. (1974) 'Export Instability and Economic Development: The Example of West Malaysia', *Oxford Economic Papers* 26, 1:78-92.

________ (1975) *Supply Responses of Primary Producers*, Kuala Lumpur: University of Malaya Press.

________ (1976) 'Export Instability and Economic Growth: A Return to Fundamentals', *Oxford Bulletin of Economics and Statistics* 38, 4:311-322.

________ (1980) 'Income Distribution, Export Instability and Savings Behaviour', *Economic Development and Cultural Change* 28, 2:359-364.

________ (1981) 'Export Instability and Revenue Instability in Less Developed Countries', *Malayan Economic Review* 26, 2:46-52.

________ (1983) 'Instability of Government Revenue and Expenditure in Less Developed Countries', *World Development* 11, 5:447-450.

________ (1987a) *Export Instability, Economic Growth and the IMF Compensatory Financing Facility: A Report for the Food and Agriculture Organisation*, Rome: FAO.

________ (1987b) 'Ability of the IMF-CFF to Stabilise Export Earnings', *Journal of World Trade Law* 21, 5:91-95.

________ (1987c) 'Export Instability, Investment and Economic Growth in Developing Countries', *Australian Economic Papers* 26, 49:318-327.

Lindert, P. and Kindleberger, C. (1982) *International Economics*, Homewood: Richard D. Irwin.

Love, J. (1979) 'Trade Concentration and Export Instability', *Journal of Development Studies* 15, 3:60-69.

________ (1987) 'Export Instability in Less Developed Countries: Consequences and Causes', *Journal of Economic Studies* 14, 2:3-80.

________ (1989) 'Export Instability, Imports and Investment in Developing Countries', *Journal of Development Studies* 25, 2:183-191.

MacBean, A.I. (1966) *Export Instability and Economic Development*, London: George Allen & Unwin.

________ and Nguyen, D.T. (1980) 'Commodity Concentration and Export Earnings: A Mathematical Analysis', *Economic Journal* 90, 358:354-362.

________ (1985) 'Compensatory Financing'. First Draft, mimeo.

Maizels, A. (1968) 'Review of Export Instability and Economic Development', *American Economic Review* 58, 3:575-580.

Marchés Tropicaux (Paris, 2 May 1985).

Massell, B. (1964) 'Export Concentration and Fluctuations in Export Earnings: A Cross-Section Analysis', *American Economic Review* 54, 2:47-63.

________ (1970) 'Export Instability and Economic Structure', *American Economic Review* 60, 4:618-630.

Michaely, M. (1962) *Concentration in International Trade*, Amsterdam: North Holland Publishing Co.

Moran, C. (1983) 'Export Fluctuations and Economic Growth', *Journal of Development Economics* 12, 1/2:195-218.

Murray, D. (1978) 'Export Earnings Instability: Price, Quantity, Supply, Demand?', *Economic Development and Cultural Change* 27, 1:61-73.

Myrdal, G. (1956) *An International Economy*, New York: Harper & Row.

Naya, S. (1973) 'Fluctuations in Export Earnings and Economic Patterns of Asian Countries', *Economic Development and Cultural Change* 21, 4:629-641.

Newbery, D.M.G. and Stiglitz, J.E. (1981) *The Theory of Commodity Price Stabilization: A Study in the Economics of Risk*, Oxford: Clarendon Press.

Nguyen, D.T. (1980) 'Partial Price Stabilization and Export Earning Instability', *Oxford Economic Papers* 32, 2:340-452.

Nurkse, R. (1953) *Problems of Capital Formation in Underdeveloped Countries*, Oxford: Basil Blackwell.

O'Brien, P. (1972) 'On Commodity Concentration of Exports in Developing Countries', *Economica Internazionale* 25, 4:160-170.

Phan-Thuy, N., Betancourt, R., Winston, G. and Kabaj, M. (1981) *Industrial Capacity and Employment Promotion*, Geneva: International Labour Organisation.

Pownall, R. and Stuart, B. (1988) 'The IMF's Compensatory and Contingency Financing Facility', *Finance and Development* 25, 4:9-11.

Priovolos, T. (1981) *Coffee and the Ivory Coast: An Econometric Study*, Lexington, Mass.: Lexington Books, D.C. Heath.

Reynolds, C.W. (1963) 'Domestic Consequences of Export Instability', *American Economic Review* 53, 2:93-102.

Sheedy, E. (1977) 'Levels and Sources of Export Instability: Some Recent Evidence', *Kyklos* 30, 2:319-324.

Soutar, G.N. (1977) 'Export Instability and Concentration in the Less Developed Countries: A Cross-Analysis', *Journal of Development Economics* 4, 3:279-297.

Stein, L. (1977) 'Export Instability and Development: A Review of Some Recent Findings', *Banco Nazionale del Lavoro Quarterly Review* 122:279-290.

Tan, G. (1983) 'Export Instability, Export Growth and GDP Growth', *Journal of Development Economics* 12, 1/2:219-227.

Treydte, K-P (1977) 'The Stabilisation of Export Earnings: Two Years' Experience in Stabex', *Intereconomics* 12, 11/12:301-305.

Turner, R.E. and Lambert, P.J. (1981) 'Commodity Concentration and Export Earnings Instability: A Comment', *Economic Journal* 91, 363:755-757.

United Nations Conference on Trade and Development (1985) *Compensatory Financing of Export Earnings Shortfalls*, New York.

________ (1981) 'Complementary Facility for Commodity-Related Shortfalls in Export Earnings: Proposal by the UNCTAD Secretariat' (TD/B/C.1/221), Geneva: UNCTAD.

________ (1986a) *Continued Analysis of the Need for a New Facility in Compensatory Financing of Export Earnings Shortfalls, as well as Further Work on the Rules and Modalities of any Additional Complementary Facility: Comments and Views by States, the Regional Commissions and Competent International Organizations on the Report of the Expert Group on Compensatory Financing of Export Earnings Shortfalls*, (TD/B/AC.43/3), Geneva: 7 April.

________ (1986b) *Continued Analysis of the Need for a New Facility in Compensatory Financing of Export Earnings Shortfalls, as well as Further Work on the Rules and Modalities of any Additional Complementary Facility: Comments and Views by States, the Regional Commissions and Competent International Organizations on the Report of the Expert Group on Compensatory Financing of Export Earnings Shortfalls*, (TD/B/AC.43/2), Geneva: 23 April.

________ (1986c) *Continued Analysis of the Need for a New Facility in Compensatory Financing of Export Earnings Shortfalls, as well as Further Work on the Rules and Modalities of any Additional Complementary Facility: Comments and Views by States, the Regional Commissions and Competent International Organizations on the Report of the Expert Group on Compensatory Financing of Export Earnings Shortfalls*, (TD/B/AC.43/3 Add 1), Geneva: 5 May.

________ (1986d) *Continued Analysis of the Need for a New Facility in Compensatory Financing of Export Earnings Shortfalls, as well as Further Work on the Rules and Modalities of any Additional Complementary Facility: Comments and Views by States, the Regional Commissions and Competent International Organizations on the Report of the Expert Group on Compensatory Financing of Export Earnings Shortfalls,* (TD/B/AC.43/3 Add 2), Geneva: 6 June.

________ (1986e) *Continued Analysis of the Need for a New Facility on Compensatory Financing of Export Earnings Shortfalls, as well as Further Work on the Rules and Modalities of any Additional Complementary Facility,* (TD/B/AC.43/L.2), 18 July.

________ (1987) *Continued Analysis of the Need for a New Facility on Compensatory Financing of Export Earnings Shortfalls, as well as Further Work on the Rules and Modalities of any Additional Complementary Facility,* (TD/B/AC.43/L.4), 18 September.

________ (1989) *Continued Analysis of the Need for a New Facility on Compensatory Financing of Export Earnings Shortfalls, as well as Further Work on the Rules and Modalities of any Additional Complementary Facility,* (TD/B/AC.43/L.6), 17 April.

United Nations, Department of Economic and Social Affairs (1951) *Measures for International Economic Stability,* New York.

United Nations, General Assembly (1975) *Official Records of the General Assembly, Seventh Special Session,* verbatim record of the 2,327th plenary meeting, New York, 1 September.

United Nations, Secretariat (1952) *Instability in the Export Markets of Under-developed Countries,* New York.

Voivodas, C. (1974) 'The Effect of Foreign Exchange Instability on Growth', *Review of Economics and Statistics* 51, 3:410-412.

Wilson, P. (1983) 'The Consequences of Export Instability for Developing Countries: A Reappraisal', *Development and Change* 14, 1:39-59.

World Bank (1965) *Supplementary Financial Measures,* Washington, D.C.

________ (1976) *World Tables 1976*, Baltimore: Johns Hopkins University Press.

________ (1986) 'World Bank Staff', in UNCTAD (1986a).

Index